WITH WORKBOOK

TOP NOTCH

English for Today's World

FUNDAMENTALS B

D1605112

WITH WORKBOOK

TOP NOTCH

English for Today's World

FUNDAMENTALS B

Joan Saslow ■ Allen Ascher

With *Top Notch Pop Songs and Karaoke*
by Rob Morsberger

PEARSON
Longman

Top Notch: English for Today's World   Fundamentals B with Workbook

Pearson Education, 10 Bank Street, White Plains, NY 10606

Editorial director: Pamela Fishman
Senior development editors: Jessica Miller-Smith, Marcia Schonzeit
Associate development editor: Siobhan Sullivan
Vice president, director of design and production: Rhea Banker
Director of electronic production: Aliza Greenblatt
Managing editor: Mike Kemper
Senior production editor: Sasha Kintzler
Production editor: Full-service production provided by Camelot Editorial Services
Art director: Ann France
Senior manufacturing buyer: Dave Dickey
Photo research: Aerin Csigay
Digital layout specialist: Warren Fischbach
Text composition: Studio Montage, Word & Image Design Studio, Inc.
Text font: Palatino 11/13, Frutiger 10/12

Photo credits: Page 74 (top) iRobot Corporation, (right) Husqvarna (U.S. Corporate Offices), (bottom) AFP/Corbis; p. 76 Gala/SuperStock; p. 85 (soup) Getty Images, (bean salad) Lisa Koenig/Stockfood America, (pancakes) Getty Images, (peppers) Solzberg Studio/Stockfood America; p. 94 (top) Photolibrary.com, (middle) Dave G. Houser/Corbis, (bottom) Fraser Hall/Robert Harding World Imagery; p. 95 (1) Bill Bachmann/Mira.com, (2) Michael Keller/Corbis, (3) Getty Images, (4) Norbert Schaefer/Corbis, (5) Tim Kiusalaas/Corbis, (6) Alamy Images; p. 96 Dennis MacDonald/PhotoEdit; p. 97 (Rome) Dallas and John Heaton/Corbis, (London) Ric Ergenbright/Corbis, (Rio) Pat Canova/Index Stock Imagery, (Moscow) H. Spichtinger/Masterfile, (Kong) Reed Kaestner/Corbis, (Hawaii) Randy Faris/Corbis, (Istanbul) Brian Lawrence/SuperStock; p. 98 (café) Catherine Karnow/Corbis, (Louvre) Walter Bibikow/Index Stock Imagery, (Tower) Royalty-Free/Corbis, (Cancun) Michele Westmorland/Corbis, (snorkeling) Mike Severns/Getty Images, (Tulum) Steve Vidler/eStock Photo, (ferry) Getty Images, (sum) Nik Wheeler/Corbis; p. 100 (3) Getty Images, (5) Getty Images, (6) Getty Images; p. 101 (Mercury) Manny Hernandez/Liaison/Getty Images, (Fat) Corbis Sygma, (Boccelli) Mencarini/Grazia Neri/Corbis Sygma, (Miguel) David Sprague/LADN/WireImage.com, (Ming) AFP/Corbis, (Binoche) Reuters NewMedia Inc./Corbis; p. 106 (Depardieu) Eric Fougere/VIP Images/Corbis, (Yi) Reuters NewMedia Inc./Corbis, (Veloso) Wrasse Records, (Reiner) Frederick M. Brown/Getty Images, (Roberts) Andrea Renault/Globe Photos; p. 111 (top left) Robert Frerck and Odyssey Productions, Inc., (middle) Bill Aron/PhotoEdit, (top right) Dave G. Houser/Corbis, (bottom left) Dennis Degnan/Corbis, (bottom right) Mimmo Jodice/Corbis; p.117 (1) Peter Beck/Corbis, (2) ATC Productions/Corbis, (3) Jose Luis Pelaez, Inc./Corbis, (4) Jose Luis Pelaez, Inc./Corbis, (5) Tom & Dee Ann McCarthy/Corbis, (6) Jose Luis Pelaez, Inc./Corbis, (7) Andrew Douglas/Masterfile, (8) Getty Images, (9) Michael Keller/Corbis, (10) Billy E. Barnes/PhotoEdit; p. 122 (Thor) Walter Leonardi, (Kon-Tiki) Getty Images; p. V1 (Unit 1) (2) Picture Quest/Jim Pickerell/Stock Connection, (3) Keith Brofsky/Getty Images, (4) Arthur S. Aubry/Getty Images, (5) Royalty-Free/Corbis, (9) Kwame Zikomo/SuperStock, (10) Royalty-Free/Corbis, (12) Jonathan Nouvok/Image Works, (16) Comstock Images, (Unit 2) (1&2) Corbis, (3) Doug Pensinger/Getty Images, (4) Royalty-Free/Corbis, (5) John Henley/Corbis, (6) Roger Ressmeyer/Corbis; p. V2 (Unit 3) (4) Vittoriano Rastelli/Corbis, (5) Corbis, (6) Corbis, (7) Corbis, (8) Tom & Dee Ann McCarthy/Corbis, (9) Tom Wagner/Corbis Saba, (10) Jeff Greenberg/PhotoEdit, (Unit 4) (1) Dorling Kindersley, (2) Duane Rieder, (3) Dorling Kindersley, (Unit 5) (1) Dorling Kindersley, (2) Corbis, (3) Dorling Kindersley, (5) Kazuhiro Nogi/AFP/Getty Images, p. V3 (3) Dorling Kindersley, (4) Comstock Images; p. V4 (19) Dorling Kindersley; p. V5 (Unit 8) (1) PhotoEdit/ Robert Brenner; p. V6 (1) A&J Verkaik/Corbis, (2) Michael S. Yamashita/Corbis, (3) Annie Griffiths Belt/National Geographic Image Collection, (4) Frozen Images/The Image Works; p. V7 (Unit 11) (2) Royalty-Free/Corbis, (Unit 12) (1) Dorling Kindersley, (2) Corbis, (3) Dorling Kindersley, (5) Royalty-Free/Corbis, (6) Royalty-Free/Corbis, (8) Royalty-Free/Corbis; p. V8 (Unit 12) (top left) Michael Keller/Corbis, (top right) Dorling Kindersley, (Unit 13) (1-11, 13) Dorling Kindersley, (12) Getty Images; p. V9 (Unit 14) (1) Douglas Faulkner/Corbis, (2) Rich Iwasaki/AGE Fotostock America, Inc., (3) Phil Schermeister/Corbis, (4) Francoise DeMulder/Corbis, (5) Jennifer W. Lester, (More) (1) Royalty-Free/Corbis, (2) Pixtal/SuperStock, (3) Royalty-Free/Corbis, (4) Tony Anderson/Getty Images, (5) Gisela Damm/eStock Photo, (6) ThinkStock/SuperStock; p. W68 Alison Wright/Corbis; p. W73 Doug Pensinger/Getty Images; p. W82 (left) Bettmann/Corbis, (right) AP Photo/Alberto Pellaschiar.

Illustration credits: Steve Attoe, p. W80; John Ceballos, pp. 83, 91, 99, 107, 115, 123; Leanne Franson, p. W49; Scott Fray, pp. 84, 87, W59; Brian Hughes, p. W84; Steve Hutchings, pp. W55, W62; Mona Mark, p. 90; Suzanne Mogensen, pp. W59, W79; Sandy Nichols, p. 79; Dusan Petričic, pp. 76, 78 (bottom), 102 (middle), 104 (top), 105, 116, 126, 130, W53 (top), W54 (bottom), W67, W87 (center, right); Mike Reagan, p.122; Phil Scheuer, pp. 70, 95 (top), 102 (bottom), 103, 104 (bottom), 108 (top), 109, 110 (bottom), 111, 118, 120, 121 (right), W53 (bottom), W54 (top), W73, W77, W85, W86, W87 (left); Jessica Miller-Smith, p. W71; Don Stewart, p. 102 (top); Neil Stewart, pp. 69, W48; Meryl Treatner, p. 114; Anna Veltfort, pp. 68, 78 (top), 88, 93, 95 (bottom), 108 (bottom), 110 (top), 112, 121 (left), 124, 129, W8, W53 (bottom), W66, W77.

Text credit: Recipes on page 90: Copyright © 1997 by Rozanne Gold. Reprinted by permission of William Morris Agency, Inc., on behalf of the Author.

ISBN: 0-13-110660-0
Printed in the United States of America
1 2 3 4 5 6 7 8 9 10–CRK–10 09 08 07 06 05

Contents

Scope and Sequence for Fundamentals A and B

UNIT	Vocabulary	Vocabulary Booster	Social Language	Grammar
1 **Names and Occupations** *Page 4*	• Occupations • The alphabet	• More occupations	• Talk about what you do • Identify people • Politely begin a conversation • Spell names	• <u>Be</u>: singular statements • Singular and plural nouns • <u>Be</u>: plural statements • <u>Be</u>: <u>yes</u> / <u>no</u> questions and short answers • Proper nouns and common nouns
2 **Relationships** *Page 12* *Top Notch* Song: "Excuse Me, Please"	• Relationships • Titles and names • Numbers 0–20	• More relationships • More titles	• Introduce people • Tell someone your first and last name • Get someone's address and phone number • Confirm information	• Possessive adjectives and nouns • <u>Be</u>: information questions with <u>What</u>
3 **Directions and Transportation** *Page 20*	• Places in the community • Locations and directions • Means of transportation	• More places in the community	• Ask about the location of places • Give and get directions • Suggest a means of transportation	• <u>Be</u>: questions with <u>Where</u> • Subject pronoun <u>it</u> • <u>There is</u> • The imperative
4 **People** *Page 28* *Top Notch* Song: "Tell Me All about It"	• Family members • Numbers 20–100 • Adjectives to describe people	• More adjectives to describe people	• Ask who someone is • Identify family members • Talk about your family • Ask about someone's age • Describe people	• <u>Be</u>: questions with <u>Who</u> • <u>Have</u> / <u>has</u>: affirmative statements • <u>Be</u>: questions with <u>How old</u> • Adjectives • <u>Very</u> and <u>so</u>
5 **Events and Times** *Page 36*	• Time • <u>Early</u>, <u>on time</u>, <u>late</u> • Events • Days of the week • Months of the year • Ordinal numbers	• More events	• Talk about time • Ask if you are late • Reassure someone • Invite someone to an event • Suggest a time to meet • Talk about dates • Ask about birthdays	• <u>Be</u>: questions about time • Prepositions of time and place
6 **Clothes** *Page 44*	• Clothes • Verbs <u>want</u>, <u>have</u>, <u>need</u> • Colors and other descriptive adjectives	• More clothes	• Give and accept compliments about clothes • Compare opinions about clothes • Talk about shopping for clothes • Describe clothes • Talk about wants and needs	• <u>This</u>, <u>that</u>, <u>these</u>, <u>those</u> • The simple present tense: affirmative statements • The simple present tense: statements and <u>yes</u> / <u>no</u> questions • Adjectives • The simple present tense: information questions
7 **Home and Work** *Page 52*	• Workplaces and homes • Rooms in the home • Furniture and appliances in the home and office	• More home and office vocabulary	• Talk about where you live, work, or study • Describe your home • Compare opinions	• Prepositions of place • <u>There is</u> and <u>There are</u> • <u>A lot of</u>

Speaking Activities	Pronunciation	Listening	Reading and Writing
• Read letters of the alphabet aloud • Spelling bee: Say and spell occupations	• Syllables	• List of letters Task: Circle the letter you hear • Conversations about names Task: Identify correct spelling and write each name • Lists of and conversations about occupations Task: Identify the correct occupation • Conversations about names and occupations Task: Listen for and write missing information	Reading • Names and occupations • Simple forms and business cards Writing • Write proper and common nouns • Complete a form with name and occupation • Write responses to statements and questions
• Ask for someone's first and last name in order to fill out a form • Read aloud a series of numbers for a partner to write • Ask and answer questions about occupations, phone numbers, addresses, and country of origin	• Stress in two-word pairs	• Introductions Task: Listen for and write relationships • Questions about first and last names Task: Circle the first or last name • Conversations about names and phone numbers Task: Write the phone number	Reading • Article about famous people, their occupations, and country of origin Writing • Fill in a form with your first name, last name, title • Fill in a form with a partner's first name and last name • Write telephone numbers from a listening
• Use a map to give location or directions • Give directions to places in your city or town	• Rising intonation to confirm	• List of places in the community Task: Number the places • Conversations about directions Task: Write the name of the place	Reading • Guide to museums around the world Writing • Write questions and answers about location • Write names of places from a listening • Write directions • List places in your city or town • Answer questions about a reading
• Read aloud numbers for a partner to circle • Interview a partner about his or her family	• Numbers	• Identifications of family members Task: Identify the correct person • Conversations describing family members Task: Identify the adjectives used for each	Reading • Article about famous people and their families Writing • Write questions with Who • Interview a partner and write about his or her family
• Discuss times, using a time-zone map • Say and write dates with a partner • Ask about classmates' birthdays	• Sentence stress	• Conversations about events Task: Identify the time of each event • A radio broadcast of upcoming events Task: Write events on a calendar, under correct day and time • List of dates Task: Circle the dates on a calendar	Reading • Newspaper entertainment section Writing • Write events on a calendar • Write dates as a partner says them • Answer questions, using prepositions of time and place • Write classmates' names
• Describe a partner's likes and dislikes • Discuss clothing you need, like, want, or have	• Plural nouns	• Conversations about clothing: likes, wants, needs Task: Identify statements as true or false	Reading • Newspaper ad for a sale at a clothing store Writing • Write names of clothes with this, that, these, or those • Write descriptions of clothes
• Talk about homes that you like and why	• Th	• Phone conversations about houses and apartments Task: Identify the best home for each person • Questions about furniture and appliances Task: Write the correct room for each item	Reading • Newspaper ads for houses and apartments • Descriptions of people's homes Writing • Write a description of a dream house • Write the furniture and appliances in your home • Write comparisons of your home and homes in a reading

Scope and Sequence for Fundamentals A and B

UNIT	Vocabulary	Vocabulary Booster	Social Language	Grammar
8 **Activities** *Page 68* *Top Notch* Song: "On the Weekend"	• Daily activities at home • Household chores and leisure activities	• More household chores	• Describe your daily activities • Tell why you are a morning person or an evening person • Describe your schedule • Talk about how often you do things • Greet an acquaintance you haven't seen in a while	• The simple present tense: spelling rules for the third-person singular • The simple present tense: habitual activities • Questions with <u>How often</u> • Frequency adverbs
9 **Weather and Ongoing Activities** *Page 76*	• Weather • Time expressions	• More weather	• Ask about the weather • Describe today's weather • Ask about people's activities • Make a polite phone call • Offer to call back later • Discuss plans • Make plans to get together	• The present continuous: affirmative and negative statements • The present continuous: <u>yes</u> / <u>no</u> questions • The present continuous: information questions • The present participle: spelling rules • The present continuous: continuing activities and future plans
10 **Food** *Page 84*	• Foods: count nouns • Places to keep food in a kitchen • Drinks and foods: non-count nouns • Containers and quantities	• More vegetables • More fruits	• Get ingredients for a recipe • Discuss what to cook • Offer and ask for foods at the table • Talk about present-time activities • Invite someone to join you	• <u>How many</u> and <u>Are there any</u> • Non-count nouns • <u>How much</u> and <u>Is there any</u> • The present continuous and the simple present tense
11 **Past Events** *Page 92* *Top Notch* Song: "My Favorite Day"	• Past-time expressions • Years • Weekend activities • Seasons	• More weekend activities	• Talk about the past • Express regret • Discuss past activities • Ask about and describe a vacation	• The past tense of <u>be</u> • The simple past tense • The simple past tense: questions
12 **Appearance and Health** *Page 100*	• Adjectives to describe hair • The face • Parts of the body • Accidents and injuries • Ailments • Remedies	• More parts of the body	• Describe people • Ask about someone who looks familiar • Show concern about an injury • Talk about an ailment • Suggest a remedy	• Use of adjectives for physical description • <u>Should</u> for advice
13 **Abilities and Requests** *Page 108*	• Abilities and skills • Adverbs to describe ability • Reasons to decline an invitation • Requests	• More musical instruments	• Discuss abilities • Decline an invitation • Request a favor	• <u>Can</u> and <u>can't</u> • <u>Too</u> + adjective • Requests with <u>Could</u> or <u>Can</u>
14 **Past, Present, and Future Plans** *Page 116* *Top Notch* Song: "I Wasn't Born Yesterday"	• Academic subjects • Life events • Free-time activities	• More academic subjects • More free-time activities	• Get to know someone's life story • Talk about where you were born • Announce good news and bad news • Congratulate someone • Ask about free-time activities • Ask about future plans	• <u>Would like</u> • <u>Be going to</u> for the future • Conditions and results in the future

Speaking Activities	Pronunciation	Listening	Reading and Writing
• Interview a partner about daily activities • Discuss how often you do things and report to the class • Talk about likes and wants in the context of a reading on robots who do housework	• Third-person singular verbs in the simple present tense	• Conversations about household chores Task: Identify the correct choice to complete sentences • Interviews about transportation Task: Complete a chart, identifying how each person gets to work or school	Reading • Article about robots that perform household chores Writing • Write sentences about daily activities • Write about a partner's daily activities • Fill in a weekly schedule • Write sentences about habitual activities • Write sentences about a reading, using the simple present tense
• Describe the weather • Ask and answer questions about activities in progress now • Charades: ask questions in the present continuous • Make plans to meet	• Rising and falling intonation of questions	• World weather broadcast Task: Write the weather and temperature for each city • Conversations about actions in progress Task: Complete sentences	Reading • A weekly date book • Instant messages Writing • Fill in a weekly date book • Write sentences about your future plans
• Ask and answer questions with How many and Are there any • Create and describe a recipe	• Vowel sounds	• Conversations about food Task: Identify the foods in each	Reading • Recipes • Weekly schedule Writing • Complete a chart with things you eat and drink • Write sentences about activities in progress and habitual activities • Write ingredients for your own recipe
• Tell a partner what you did yesterday • Discuss your favorite season • Ask questions about past activities • Talk about where you want to go on vacation • Describe a vacation you took	• The simple past tense ending	• List of years Task: Identify the correct year • Conversations about events Task: Complete sentences about the day or month of each event	Reading • Descriptions of vacations Writing • Write sentences about past activities • Write sentences to answer questions about a reading • Write a description of a past vacation
• Game: Practice "Parts of the body" vocabulary • Guessing game: describe a classmate	• Back-vowel sounds	• Descriptions of hair Task: Identify the people described • Conversations about injuries Task: Write the injuries • Conversations about ailments Task: Identify the ailments	Reading • Descriptions of people Writing • Write sentences suggesting remedies • Write a description of a classmate
• Describe your abilities • Discuss things children can and can't do at different ages	• Can and can't	• Requests Task: Identify the picture to match each request	Reading • Article about infant and toddler abilities Writing • Write sentences with too and an adjective • Complete sentences about abilities, based on a reading
• Interview a partner about his or her past • Compare plans for the future • Present a short history of your life	• Diphthongs	• An interview about someone's childhood Task: Check the statements that are true • Conversations about future free-time activities Task: Complete sentences with the activities	Reading • Article about Thor Heyerdahl Writing • Write about a partner's life story • Write statements about future plans • Write statements and questions with be going to • Write sentences about a partner's future plans • Write answers to questions, based on a reading • Write a short history of your life

Acknowledgments

Top Notch International Advisory Board

The authors gratefully acknowledge the substantive and formative contributions of the members of the International Advisory Board.

CHERYL BELL, Middlesex County College, Middlesex, New Jersey, USA • **ELMA CABAHUG**, City College of San Francisco, San Francisco, California, USA • **JO CARAGATA**, Mukogawa Women's University, Hyogo, Japan • **ANN CARTIER**, Palo Alto Adult School, Palo Alto, California, USA • **TERRENCE FELLNER**, Himeji Dokkyo University, Hyogo, Japan • **JOHN FUJIMORI**, Meiji Gakuin High School, Tokyo, Japan • **ARETA ULHANA GALAT**, Escola Superior de Estudos Empresariais e Informática, Curitiba, Brazil • **DOREEN M. GAYLORD**, Kanazawa Technical College, Ishikawa, Japan • **EMILY GEHRMAN**, Newton International College, Garden Grove, California, USA • **ANN-MARIE HADZIMA**, National Taiwan University, Taipei, Taiwan • **KAREN KYONG-AI PARK**, Seoul National University, Seoul, Korea • **ANA PATRICIA MARTÍNEZ VITE DIP. R.S.A.**, Universidad del Valle de México, Mexico City, Mexico • **MICHELLE ANN MERRITT**, Proulex/ Universidad de Guadalajara, Guadalajara, Mexico • **ADRIANNE P. OCHOA**, Georgia State University, Atlanta, Georgia, USA • **LOUIS PARDILLO**, Korea Herald English Institute, Seoul, Korea • **THELMA PERES**, Casa Thomas Jefferson, Brasilia, Brazil • **DIANNE RUGGIERO**, Broward Community College, Davie, Florida, USA • **KEN SCHMIDT**, Tohoku Fukushi University, Sendai, Japan • **ALISA A. TAKEUCHI**, Garden Grove Adult Education, Garden Grove, California, USA • **JOSEPHINE TAYLOR**, Centro Colombo Americano, Bogotá, Colombia • **PATRICIA VECIÑO**, Instituto Cultural Argentino Norteamericano, Buenos Aires, Argentina • **FRANCES WESTBROOK**, AUA Language Center, Bangkok, Thailand

Reviewers and Piloters
Many thanks also to the reviewers and piloters all over the world who reviewed *Top Notch* in its final form.

G. Julian Abaqueta, Huachiew Chalermprakiet University, Samutprakarn, Thailand • **David Aline**, Kanagawa University, Kanagawa, Japan • **Marcia Alves**, Centro Cultural Brasil Estados Unidos, Franca, Brazil • **Yousef Al-Yacoub**, Qatar Petroleum, Doha, Qatar • **Maristela Barbosa Silveira e Silva**, Instituto Cultural Brasil-Estados Unidos, Manaus, Brazil • **Beth Bartlett**, Centro Colombo Americano, Cali, Colombia • **Carla Battigelli**, University of Zulia, Maracaibo, Venezuela • **Claudia Bautista**, C.B.C., Caracas, Venezuela • **Rob Bell**, Shumei Yachiyo High School, Chiba, Japan • **Dr. Maher Ben Moussa**, Sharjah University, Sharjah, United Arab Emirates • **Elaine Cantor**, Englewood Senior High School, Jacksonville, Florida, USA • **María Aparecida Capellari**, SENAC, São Paulo, Brazil • **Eunice Carrillo Ramos**, Colegio Durango, Naucalpan, Mexico • **Janette Carvalhinho de Oliveira**, Centro de Linguas (UFES), Vitória, Brazil • **María Amelia Carvalho Fonseca**, Centro Cultural Brasil-Estados Unidos, Belém, Brazil • **Audy Castañeda**, Instituto Pedagógico de Caracas, Caracas, Venezuela • **Ching-Fen Chang**, National Chiao Tung University, Hsinchu, Taiwan • **Ying-Yu Chen**, Chinese Culture University, Taipei, Taiwan • **Joyce Chin**, The Language Training and Testing Center, Taipei, Taiwan • **Eun Cho**, Pagoda Language School, Seoul, Korea • **Hyungzung Cho**, MBC Language Institute, Seoul, Korea • **Dong Sua Choi**, MBC Language Institute, Seoul, Korea • **Jeong Mi Choi**, Freelancer, Seoul, Korea • **Peter Chun**, Pagoda Language School, Seoul, Korea • **Eduardo Corbo**, Legacy ELT, Salto, Uruguay • **Marie Cosgrove**, Surugadai University, Saitama, Japan • **María Antonieta Covarrubias Souza**, Centro Escolar Akela, Mexico City, Mexico • **Katy Cox**, Casa Thomas Jefferson, Brasilia, Brazil • **Michael Donovan**, Gakushuin University, Tokyo, Japan • **Stewart Dorward**, Shumei Eiko High School, Saitama, Japan • **Ney Eric Espina**, Centro Venezolano Americano del Zulia, Maracaibo, Venezuela • **Edith Espino**, Centro Especializado de Lenguas - Universidad Tecnológica de Panamá, El Dorado, Panama • **Allen P. Fermon**, Instituto Brasil-Estados Unidos, Ceará, Brazil • **Simão Ferreira Banha**, Phil Young's English School, Curitiba, Brazil • **María Elena Flores Lara**, Colegio Mercedes, Mexico City, Mexico • **Valesca Fróis Nassif**, Associação Cultural Brasil-Estados Unidos, Salvador, Brazil • **José Fuentes**, Empire Language Consulting, Caracas, Venezuela • **Claudia Patricia Gutiérrez**, Centro Colombo Americano, Cali, Colombia • **Valerie Hansford**, Asia University, Tokyo, Japan • **Gene Hardstark**, Dotkyo University, Saitama, Japan • **Maiko Hata**, Kansai University, Osaka, Japan • **Susan Elizabeth Haydock Miranda de Araujo**, Centro Cultural Brasil Estados Unidos, Belém, Brazil • **Gabriela Herrera**, Fundametal, Valencia, Venezuela • **Sandy Ho**, GEOS International, New York, New York, USA • **Yuri Hosoda**, Showa Women's University, Tokyo, Japan • **Hsiao-I Hou**, Shu-Te University, Kaohsiung County, Taiwan • **Kuei-ping Hsu**, National Tsing Hua University, Hsinchu, Taiwan • **Chia-yu Huang**, National Tsing Hua University, Hsinchu, Taiwan • **Caroline C. Hwang**, National Taipei University of Science and Technology, Taipei, Taiwan • **Eunjeong Kim**, Freelancer, Seoul, Korea • **Julian Charles King**, Qatar Petroleum, Doha, Qatar • **Bruce Lee**, CIE: Foreign Language Institute, Seoul, Korea • **Myunghee Lee**, MBC Language Institute, Seoul, Korea • **Naidnapa Leoprasertkul**, Language Development Center, Mahasarakham University, Mahasarakham, Thailand • **Eleanor S. Leu**, Souchow University, Taipei, Taiwan • **Eliza Liu**, Chinese Culture University, Taipei, Taiwan • **Philippe Loussarevian**, Keio University Shonan Fujisawa High School, Kanagawa, Japan • **Jonathan Lynch**, Azabu University, Tokyo, Japan • **Thomas Mach**, Konan University, Hyogo, Japan • **Lilian Mandel Civatti**, Associação Cultural Brasil-Estados Unidos, Salvador, Brazil • **Hakan Mansuroglu**, Zoni Language Center, West New York, New Jersey, USA • **Martha McGaughey**, Language Training Institute, Englewood Cliffs, New Jersey, USA • **David Mendoza Plascencia**, Instituto Internacional de Idiomas, Naucalpan, Mexico • **Theresa Mezo**, Interamerican University, Río Piedras, Puerto Rico • **Luz Adriana Montenegro Silva**, Colegio CAFAM, Bogotá, Colombia • **Magali de Moraes Menti**, Instituto Lingua, Porto Alegre, Brazil • **Massoud Moslehpour**, The Overseas Chinese Institute of Technology, Taichung, Taiwan • **Jennifer Nam**, IKE, Seoul, Korea • **Marcos Norelle F. Victor**, Instituto Brasil-Estados Unidos, Ceará, Brazil • **Luz María Olvera**, Instituto Juventud del Estado de México, Naucalpan, Mexico • **Roxana Orrego Ramírez**, Universidad Diego Portales, Santiago, Chile • **Ming-Jong Pan**, National Central University, Jhongli City, Taiwan • **Sandy Park**, Topia Language School, Seoul, Korea • **Patrícia Elizabeth Peres Martins**, Instituto Brasil-Estados Unidos, Rio de Janeiro, Brazil • **Rodrigo Peza**, Passport Language Centers, Bogotá, Colombia • **William Porter**, Osaka Institute of Technology, Osaka, Japan • **Caleb Prichard**, Kwansei Gakuin University, Hyogo, Japan • **Mirna Quintero**, Instituto Pedagógico de Caracas, Caracas, Venezuela • **Roberto Rabbini**, Seigakuin University, Saitama, Japan • **Terri Rapoport**, Berkeley College, White Plains, New York, USA • **Yvette Rieser**, Centro Electrónico de Idiomas, Maracaibo, Venezuela • **Orlando Rodríguez**, New English Teaching School, Paysandu, Uruguay • **Mayra Rosario**, Pontificia Universidad Católica Madre y Maestra, Santiago, Dominican Republic • **Peter Scout**, Sakura no Seibo Junior College, Fukushima, Japan • **Jungyeon Shim**, EG School, Seoul, Korea • **Keum Ok Song**, MBC Language Institute, Seoul, Korea • **Assistant Professor Dr. Reongrudee Soonthornmanee**, Chulalongkorn University Language Institute, Bangkok, Thailand • **Claudia Stanisclause**, The Language College, Maracay, Venezuela • **Tom Suh**, The Princeton Review, Seoul, Korea • **Phiphawin Suphawat**, KhonKaen University, KhonKaen, Thailand • **Craig Sweet**, Poole Gakuin Junior and Senior High Schools, Osaka, Japan • **Yi-nien Josephine Twu**, National Tsing Hua University, Hsinchu, Taiwan • **Maria Christina Uchôa Close**, Instituto Cultural Brasil-Estados Unidos, São José dos Campos, Brazil • **Luz Vanegas Lopera**, Lexicom The Place For Learning English, Medellín, Colombia • **Julieta Vasconcelos García**, Centro Escolar del Lago, A.C., Mexico City, Mexico • **Carol Vaughan**, Kanto Kokusai High School, Tokyo, Japan • **Patricia Celia Veciño**, Instituto Cultural Argentino Norteamericano, Buenos Aires, Argentina • **Isabela Villas Boas**, Casa Thomas Jefferson, Brasilia, Brazil • **Iole Vitti**, Peanuts English School, Poços de Caldas, Brazil • **Gabi Witthaus**, Qatar Petroleum, Doha, Qatar • **Yi-Ling Wu**, Shih Chien University, Taipei, Taiwan • **Chad Wynne**, Osaka Keizai University, Osaka, Japan • **Belkis Yanes**, Freelance Instructor, Caracas, Venezuela • **I-Chieh Yang**, Chung-kuo Institute of Technology, Taipei, Taiwan • **Emil Ysona**, Instituto Cultural Dominico-Americano, Santo Domingo, Dominican Republic • **Chi-fang Yu**, Soo Chow University, Taipei, Taiwan, • **Shigeki Yusa**, Sendai Shirayuri Women's College, Sendai, Japan

To the Teacher

What is *Top Notch?*

- *Top Notch* is a six-level communicative English course for adults and young adults, with two beginning entry levels.
- *Top Notch* prepares students to interact successfully and confidently with both native and non-native speakers of English.
- *Top Notch* demonstrably brings students to a "Top Notch" level of communicative competence.

Key Elements of the *Top Notch* Instructional Design

Concise two-page lessons

Each easy-to-teach two-page lesson is designed for one class session and begins with a clearly stated communication goal and ends with controlled or free communication practice. Each lesson provides vocabulary, grammar, and social language contextualized in all four skills, keeping the pace of a class session lively and varied.

Daily confirmation of progress

Adult and young adult students need to observe and confirm their own progress. In *Top Notch*, students conclude each class session with a controlled or free practice activity that demonstrates their ability to use new vocabulary, grammar, and social language. This motivates and keeps students eager to continue their study of English and builds their pride in being able to speak accurately, fluently, and authentically.

Real language

Carefully exposing students to authentic, natural English, both receptively and productively, is a necessary component of building understanding and expression. All conversation models feature the language people really use; nowhere to be found is "textbook English" written merely to exemplify grammar.

Practical content

In addition to classic topical vocabulary, grammar, and conversation, *Top Notch* includes systematic practice of highly practical language, such as: how to advise someone on whether to take a bus or taxi, how to ask for foods at the table, how to compliment someone on their clothes, how to tell a friend about your weekend—usable language today's students want and need.

Memorable model conversations

Effective language instruction must make language memorable. The full range of social and functional communicative needs is presented through practical model conversations that are intensively practiced and manipulated, first within a guided model and then in freer and more personalized formats.

High-impact vocabulary syllabus

In order to ensure students' solid acquisition of vocabulary essential for communication, *Top Notch* contains explicit presentation, practice, and systematic extended recycling of words, collocations, and expressions appropriate at each level of study. The extensive captioned illustrations, photos, definitions, examples, and contextualized sentences remove doubts about meaning and provide a permanent in-book reference for student test preparation. An added benefit is that teachers don't have to search for pictures to bring to class and don't have to resort to translating vocabulary into the students' native language.

Learner-supportive grammar

Grammar is approached explicitly and cognitively, through form, meaning, and use. Charts provide examples and paradigms enhanced by simple usage notes at students' level of comprehension. This takes the guesswork out of meaning, makes lesson preparation easier for teachers, and provides students with comprehensible charts for permanent reference and test preparation. All presentations of grammar are followed by exercises to ensure adequate practice.

English as an international language

Top Notch prepares students for interaction with both native and non-native speakers of English, both linguistically and culturally. English is treated as an international language, rather than the language of a particular country or region. In addition, *Top Notch* helps students develop a cultural fluency by creating an awareness of the varied rules across cultures for: politeness, greetings and introductions, appropriateness of dress in different settings, conversation do's and taboos, table manners, and other similar issues.

Two beginning-level texts

Beginning students can be placed either in *Top Notch 1* or *Top Notch Fundamentals*, depending on ability and background. Even absolute beginners can start with confidence in *Top Notch Fundamentals*. False beginners can begin with *Top Notch 1*. The *Top Notch Placement Test* clarifies the best placement within the series.

Estimated teaching time

Each level of *Top Notch* is designed for 60 to 90 instructional hours and contains a full range of supplementary components and enrichment devices to tailor the course to individual needs.

Components of *Top Notch Fundamentals*

Student's Book

The Student's Book contains a bound-in Vocabulary Booster and Student's Take-Home Audio CD with pronunciation/intonation practice and the *Top Notch Pop* songs.

Teacher's Edition and Lesson Planner

Complete yet concise lesson plans are provided for each class. Corpus notes provide essential information from the *Longman Spoken American Corpus* and the *Longman Learner's Corpus*. In addition, a free Teacher's Resource Disk offers the following printable extension activities to personalize your teaching style:

- Grammar self-checks
- *Top Notch Pop* song activities
- Writing process worksheets
- Learning strategies
- Pronunciation activities and supplements
- Extra reading comprehension activities
- Vocabulary cards and cumulative vocabulary activities
- Graphic organizers
- Pair work cards

Copy & Go: Ready-made Interactive Activities for Busy Teachers

Interactive games, puzzles, and other practice activities in convenient photocopiable form support the Student's Book content and provide a welcome change of pace.

Complete Classroom Audio Program

The audio program contains listening comprehension activities, rhythm and intonation practice, and targeted pronunciation activities that focus on accurate and comprehensible pronunciation.

Because *Top Notch* prepares students for international communication, a variety of native and non-native speakers are included to ready students for the world outside the classroom. The audio program also includes the five *Top Notch Pop* songs in standard and karaoke form.

Workbook

A tightly linked illustrated Workbook contains exercises that provide additional practice and reinforcement of language concepts and skills from *Top Notch* and its Vocabulary Booster.

Complete Assessment Package with *ExamView®* Software

Fourteen easy-to-administer and easy-to-score unit achievement tests assess listening, vocabulary, grammar, social language, reading, and writing. Two review tests, one mid-book and one end-of-book, provide additional cumulative assessment. Two speaking tests assess progress in speaking. In addition to the photocopiable achievement tests, *ExamView®* software enables teachers to tailor-make tests to best meet their needs by combining items in any way they wish.

Top Notch TV

A lively and entertaining video offers a TV-style situation comedy that reintroduces language from each *Top Notch* unit, plus authentic unrehearsed interviews with English speakers from around the world and authentic Karaoke. Packaged with the video are activity worksheets and a booklet with teaching suggestions and complete video scripts.

Companion Website

A Companion Website at www.longman.com/topnotch provides numerous additional resources for students and teachers. This no-cost, high-benefit feature includes opportunities for further practice of language and content from the *Top Notch* Student's Book.

Welcome to Top Notch!

About the Authors

Joan Saslow

Joan Saslow has taught English as a Foreign Language and English as a Second Language to adults and young adults in both South America and the United States. She taught English and French at the Binational Centers of Valparaíso and Viña del Mar, Chile, and the Catholic University of Valparaíso. Ms. Saslow taught English as a Foreign Language to Japanese university students at Marymount College and to international students in Westchester Community College's intensive English program as well as workplace English at the General Motors auto assembly plant in Tarrytown, NY.

Ms. Saslow is the series director of Longman's popular five-level adult series *True Colors: An EFL Course for Real Communication* and of *True Voices*, a five-level video course. She is author of *Ready to Go: Language, Lifeskills, and Civics*, a four-level adult ESL series; *Workplace Plus*, a vocational English series; and of *Literacy Plus*, a two-level series that teaches literacy, English, and culture to adult pre-literate students. She is also author of *English in Context: Reading Comprehension for Science and Technology*, a three-level series for English for special purposes. In addition, Ms. Saslow has been an author, an editor of language teaching materials, a teacher-trainer, and a frequent speaker at gatherings of EFL and ESL teachers for over thirty years.

Allen Ascher

Allen Ascher has been a teacher and teacher-trainer in both China and the United States, as well as an administrator and a publisher. Mr. Ascher specialized in teaching listening and speaking to students at the Beijing Second Foreign Language Institute, to hotel workers at a major international hotel in China, and to Japanese students from Chubu University studying English at Ohio University. In New York, Mr. Ascher taught students of all language backgrounds and abilities at the City University of New York and he trained teachers in the TESOL Certificate Program at the New School. He was also the academic director of the International English Language Institute at Hunter College.

Mr. Ascher has provided lively workshops for EFL teachers throughout Asia, Latin America, Europe, and the Middle East. He is author of the popular *Think about Editing: A Grammar Editing Guide for ESL Writers*. As a publisher, Mr. Ascher played a key role in the creation of some of the most widely used materials for adults, including: *True Colors, NorthStar, Focus on Grammar, Global Links*, and *Ready to Go*. Mr. Ascher has an MA in Applied Linguistics from Ohio University.

UNIT **8**

Activities

UNIT GOALS
1 Describe your daily activities
2 Describe your schedule
3 Talk about how often you do things

LESSON 1

Describe Your Daily Activities

A 🎧 **VOCABULARY.** Daily activities at home. **Listen and practice.**

1. get up

2. get dressed

3. brush my teeth

4. comb / brush my hair

5. shave

6. put on my makeup

7. eat breakfast

8. come home

9. make dinner

10. get undressed

11. take a shower / a bath

12. watch TV

13. go to bed

🎧 **MEALS**
breakfast
lunch
dinner

B **GRAMMAR.** The simple present tense: spelling rules with <u>he</u>, <u>she</u>, <u>it</u>

Add **-s** to most verbs with <u>he</u>, <u>she</u>, and <u>it</u>.

    get**s**   make**s**   shave**s**   comb**s**   play**s**

Add **-es** to verbs that end in -<u>s</u>, -<u>sh</u>, -<u>ch</u>, or -<u>x</u>.

    bru<u>sh**es**</u>   wat<u>ch**es**</u>

But remember: do → **does**   go → **goes**   have → **has**   study → **studies**

C 🎧 **PRONUNCIATION.** Third-person singular verbs in the simple present tense. **Listen and practice the final sound of each word.**

1. /s/	**2.** /z/	**3.** /ɪz/
gets = get/s/	**shave**s = shave/z/	**watch**es = watch/ɪz/
takes = take/s/	**come**s = come/z/	**brush**es = brush/ɪz/
eats = eat/s/	**need**s = need/z/	**practice**s = practice/ɪz/

D Complete the sentences with daily activity verbs in the simple present tense. Then read the sentences aloud.

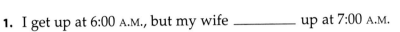

Before and after

before 8:00   at 8:00   after 8:00

1. I get up at 6:00 A.M., but my wife _____ up at 7:00 A.M.
2. My wife _____ breakfast at 7:30.
3. When my wife is late for work, she _____ on her makeup on the train.
4. I don't watch TV, but my wife _____ TV after dinner.

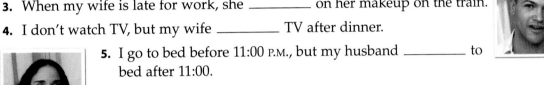

5. I go to bed before 11:00 P.M., but my husband _____ to bed after 11:00.
6. I take a bath every morning, but my husband _____ a shower.
7. I make the bed on weekdays, and my husband _____ the bed on the weekend.
8. I brush my teeth twice a day, but my husband _____ his teeth three times a day.

E **WHAT ABOUT YOU?** On a separate piece of paper, write sentences about what you and the people in your family do every day.

CONVERSATION • *Describe your daily activities.*

1. **MODEL.** **Read and listen.**

Yuka: Are you a morning person or an evening person?

Melody: Me? I'm definitely an evening person.

Yuka: Why do you say that?

Melody: Well, I get up after ten. And I go to bed after two. What about you?

Yuka: I'm a morning person. I get up at six.

2. **Rhythm and intonation practice**

3. **PAIR WORK.** Compare your daily activities with a partner. Use the guide, or create a new conversation.

A: Are you a morning person or an evening person?

B: Me? I'm _____.

A: _____ . . .

Continue the conversation about other daily activities.

69

Describe Your Schedule

LESSON 2

A 🎧 **VOCABULARY.** Household chores and leisure activities. **Listen and practice.**

Household chores

1. wash the dishes
2. clean the house
3. do the laundry
4. take out the garbage
5. go shopping

Leisure activities

6. exercise
7. take a nap
8. listen to music
9. read
10. play soccer
11. check e-mail

📖 **VOCABULARY BOOSTER** See page V5 for more.

B 🎧 **LISTENING COMPREHENSION.** **Listen to the conversations about household chores. Circle the correct choice.**

1. Marie _____.
   a. cleans the apartment
   b. washes the dishes

2. Paul _____.
   a. takes out the garbage
   b. washes the dishes

3. Sue's brother _____.
   a. takes out the garbage
   b. does the laundry

4. Jen's husband _____.
   a. washes the dishes
   b. takes out the garbage

C **GRAMMAR.** The simple present tense: habitual activities

Use the simple present tense for habitual activities.

She checks her e-mail **every day**.

M	T	W	T	F	S	S
✓	✓	✓	✓	✓	✓	✓

He goes shopping **on Saturdays**.

M	T	W	T	F	S	S
					✓	
					✓	

Other time expressions

	M	T	W	T	F	S	S
once a week			✓				
twice a week			✓	✓			
three times a week			✓	✓		✓	

D **PAIR WORK.** Ask your partner the questions. Add your own questions. Then write about your partner.

- When do you do the laundry?
- What do you do on the weekend?
- When does your family go shopping for food?
- When do you watch TV?

Alex does the laundry on Sundays.

CONVERSATION • *Describe your schedule.*

1. 🎧 **MODEL.** Read and listen.

Andy: What's your typical week like?

Sasha: Well, on Mondays and Wednesdays I go to school.

Andy: And what about the other days?

Sasha: On Tuesdays and Thursdays I work.

Andy: Sounds like you're pretty busy.

Sasha: Yes, I am. What about you?

Andy: I work every weekday. On the weekend I exercise and go to the movies.

2. 🎧 **Rhythm and intonation practice**

3. **PAIR WORK.** Write <u>your</u> typical weekly activities on the schedule. Then discuss your weekly schedules. Start like this:

A: What's your typical week like?

B: Well, _____.

A: And what about _____?

B: _____ . . .

Continue in your <u>own</u> way . . .

Monday

Tuesday

Wednesday

Thursday

Friday

Saturday

Sunday

3 ▷ Talk about How Often You Do Things

A **GRAMMAR.** Questions with <u>How often</u> / frequency adverbs ———

Use <u>How often</u> to ask about frequency.

<u>How often</u> do you go out for dinner?   About three times a week.

<u>How often</u> does she visit her parents?   Every weekend.

Use frequency adverbs with the simple present tense.

100%   always
  usually
  sometimes
0%   never

I **always take** the bus to work.
Do you **usually take** the train to work?
He **sometimes exercises** in the morning.
My brother and his wife **never go** to concerts.

B 🎧 **LISTENING COMPREHENSION.** Listen to the interviews about how people get to work and school. Complete the chart. Then listen again to check your work.

	Lynn	Matt	Jess	Frank
walks	☐	☐	☐	☐
drives	☐	☐	☐	☐
takes the bus	☐	☐	☐	☐
takes the train	☐	☐	☐	☐
takes a taxi	☐	☐	☐	☐

C **WHAT ABOUT YOU?** Write answers with frequency adverbs.

I usually walk to work.

1. How do you go to school or work? _____.
2. When do you eat lunch and dinner? _____.
3. Do you take a nap in the afternoon? _____.

D **PAIR WORK.** Ask your partner questions. Complete the chart. Then tell the class about your partner.

How often do you:	You	Your partner
do the laundry?		
make dinner?		
go out for dinner?		
go to the movies?		
go dancing?		
practice speaking English?		

CONVERSATION • *Talk about how often you do things.*

1. 🎧 **MODEL.** **Read and listen.**

Bruce: Hi, Kevin. Long time no see.
Kevin: Hi, Bruce.
Bruce: Do you always take the bus?
Kevin: No, I usually walk.
Bruce: No wonder I never see you!

2. 🎧 **Rhythm and intonation practice**

3. **PAIR WORK.** Role-play running into a friend. Use the pictures and the guide, or create a new conversation.

A: Hi, _____. Long time no see.
B: Hi, _____.
A: Do you always _____?
B: No, I usually _____.
A: No wonder I never see you!

A 🎧 **READING.** Read and listen. Do you like housework?

Don't like housework?
CHECK OUT THESE NEW ROBOTS . . .

This is the iRobot Roomba Intelligent FloorVac®, or Roomba®. The Roomba is the world's first robot vacuum cleaner. How often do you clean your house? Once a week? The Roomba vacuums your rooms for you. You turn it on and it vacuums while you watch TV, exercise, or listen to music. Or while you sleep! The Roomba

Roomba

goes straight and it turns left or right. It turns if there is a sofa or a chair.

"Excellent! This is such a great idea!"
Judy Ruvo, New Zealand

This is the Auto Mower®. It's a robot that mows the lawn. You tell the robot what time you want it to work. How about after midnight, after you go to bed? It mows the lawn while you sleep. Or how about at noon? It mows the lawn while you have lunch. The Auto Mower can mow the lawn for 24 hours! Like the Roomba, it turns left and right, goes straight, and turns at the corner.

"What a robot!"
Mark Minor, U.K.

Auto Mower

Aibo

Meet Aibo®, the robot dog from SONY. Aibo doesn't vacuum. It doesn't mow the lawn. It doesn't do household chores like the laundry or the dishes. It dances and plays with a ball, and—like the Roomba and the Auto Mower—it moves around in the house or outside. Say, "Turn left," and it turns left.

"Great fun!" Chris Maverick, U.S.A.

Sources: http://www.onrobo.com, http://international.husqvarna.com, and http://www.us.aibo.com

 B **WRITING.** Write sentences about the robots. Use the simple present tense of verbs from the box.

1. *The Roomba cleans the house* .
2. _____ .
3. _____ .
4. _____ .
5. _____ .
6. _____ .

clean the house
mow the lawn
play with a ball
turn right and left
dance
do the laundry
wash the dishes

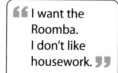 **C** **DISCUSSION.** Do you like the robots in the article? Which ones do you want? Why?

  " I want the Roomba. I don't like housework. "

🎧 *TOP NOTCH SONG*
"Excuse Me, Please"
Lyrics on last page before Workbook.

TOP NOTCH WEBSITE
For Unit 8 online activities, visit the *Top Notch* Companion Website at www.longman.com/topnotch.

- **Vocabulary.** Study the pictures. Close your book. Tell your partner all the activities you remember.
  Get up, eat breakfast . . .

- **Tell a story.** Write about Jack Benson's daily activities. Use time expressions.
  Jack Benson gets up at 7:00 on weekdays.

Jack Benson
Typical Weekday

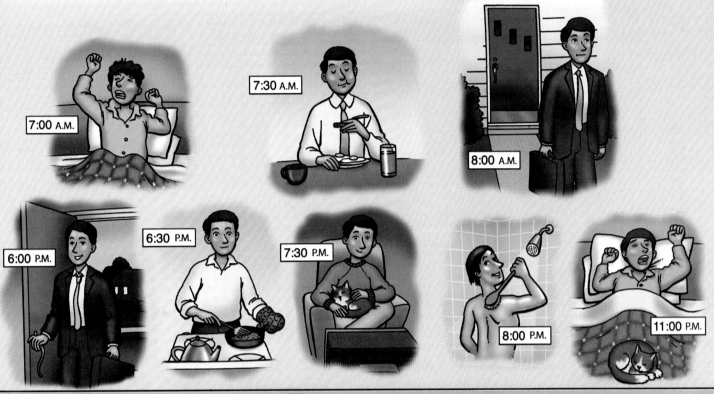

Typical Weekend

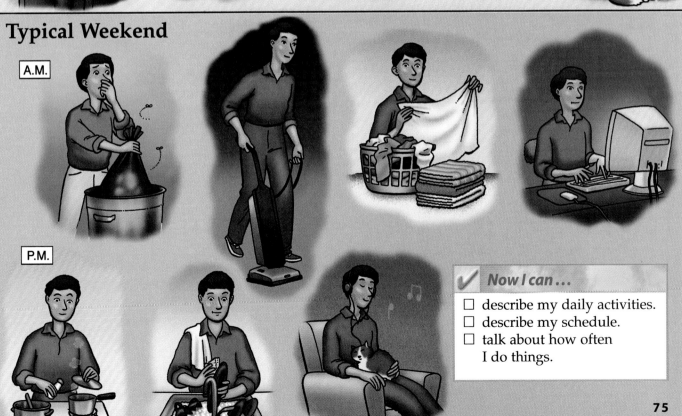

✔ **Now I can . . .**

- ☐ describe my daily activities.
- ☐ describe my schedule.
- ☐ talk about how often I do things.

UNIT 9

Weather and Ongoing Activities

UNIT GOALS

1 Describe today's weather
2 Ask about people's activities
3 Discuss plans

LESSON

1 Describe Today's Weather

A 🎧 **VOCABULARY.** What's the weather like? **Listen and practice.**

1. It's cloudy.

2. It's sunny.

6. It's hot.

7. It's cold.

3. It's windy.

4. It's raining.

5. It's snowing.

8. It's warm.

9. It's cool.

📖 **VOCABULARY BOOSTER** See page V6 for more.

B 🎧 **LISTENING COMPREHENSION.** Listen. Check ☑ today's weather in each of the cities. Then listen again. Write today's temperature.

	Hot	Warm	Cool	Cold	Temperature
Tokyo	✔				37°
London					
Mexico City					
Santiago					

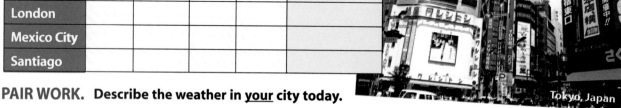

Tokyo, Japan

C **PAIR WORK.** Describe the weather in <u>your</u> city today.

D **GRAMMAR.** The present continuous: affirmative and negative statements

The present continuous expresses actions in progress now. Use a form of <u>be</u> and a present participle.

Affirmative statements

It's raining.
She's exercising today.
They're wearing sweaters.

Negative statements

It's not snowing.
She's not studying.
They're not wearing jackets.

Present participles
wear → wearing
study → studying
exercise → exercising

E ▷ **GRAMMAR.** **The present continuous:** <u>yes</u> / <u>no</u> **questions**

Are you **reading** right now?	Yes, I am.	No, I'm not.
Is he **washing** the dishes?	Yes, he is.	No, he's not. [No, he isn't.]
Is it **raining**?	Yes, it is.	No, it's not. [No, it isn't.]
Are they **eating**?	Yes, they are.	No, they're not. [No, they aren't.]

F ▷ **Complete the conversations with the present continuous.**

1. **A:** <u>Are they cleaning</u> the house?
   they / clean

   B: No, they _____. They _____ to music.
   listen

2. **A:** _____ right now?
   you / work

   B: No, we _____. We _____ TV.
   watch

3. **A:** _____ English?
   she / study

   B: No, she _____. She _____ her e-mail.
   check

4. **A:** _____ the laundry?
   Mr. and Mrs. Reed / do

   B: No, they _____. They _____ the dishes.
   wash

CONVERSATION • *Describe today's weather.*

1. **MODEL. Read and listen.**

Paul: Hi, Manny. I'm calling from San Francisco. How's the weather in Lima?

Manny: Today? Awful. It's 18 degrees and raining.

Paul: No kidding. It's hot and sunny here!

2. ⌂ **Rhythm and intonation practice**

3. **PAIR WORK. Choose two cities. Then role-play a conversation. Use the guide, or create a new conversation.**

A: Hi, _____. I'm calling from _____. How's the weather in _____?

B: Today? _____.

A: No kidding. It's _____ here!

💡 *Ideas*

Find the weather report in the newspaper. Or log onto www.weather.com.

International Express Airlines
Departures

Flight

003   Lima   7:30 A.M On Time

Information Center

77

2 | Ask about People's Activities

A 🎧 **GRAMMAR.** The present continuous: information questions

Who's driving?	Sarah is.
What are you **doing?**	Watching TV.
Where are Tim and Jack **going?**	They're going out for dinner.

B **PAIR WORK.** Ask your partner questions about Mike and Patty. Use the present continuous.

> 66 It's 8:00. What's Patty doing? 99

> 66 She's taking a shower. 99

C 🎧 **PRONUNCIATION.** Rising and falling intonation of questions. **Use rising intonation for yes / no questions. Use falling intonation for information questions. Listen and practice.**

Yes / no questions	Information questions
1. Are you reading?	What are you reading?
2. Is she driving?	Where is she driving?
3. Are they watching TV?	Who's watching TV?
4. Is your family here?	Where's your family?
5. Is there a pharmacy near here?	Where is there a pharmacy?

D **CHARADES.** One team mimes an activity. The other team asks questions. Use the activities from the box.

get up	get dressed	brush your teeth
comb your hair	take a shower	wash the dishes
drive	read	check e-mail
exercise	watch TV	listen to music
talk on the phone	go to bed	eat breakfast

> Are you combing your hair?

E ▶ **GRAMMAR.** The present participle: spelling rules

talk → **talking**	mak~~e~~ → **making**
read → **reading**	tak~~e~~ → **taking**
watch → **watching**	com~~e~~ → **coming**

But remember: shop → shopping   get → getting

F ▶ **Write the present participles.**

1. read _____

2. write _____

3. wash _____

4. go _____

5. drive _____

6. get up _____

G ▶ ⌂ **LISTENING COMPREHENSION. Listen. Complete each statement in the present continuous.**

1. She's _watching TV_ with her father.

2. He's _____.

3. She's _____ her mother.

4. He's _____ for the kids.

5. They're _____ to the museum.

CONVERSATION • *Make a polite phone call.*

1. ⌂ **MODEL. Read and listen.**

Jan: Hello?

Laura: Hi, Jan. This is Laura. What are you doing?

Jan: I'm feeding the kids.

Laura: Should I call you back later?

Jan: Yes, thanks. Talk to you later. Bye.

Laura: Bye.

2. ⌂ **Rhythm and intonation practice**

3. **PAIR WORK. Now role-play a call. Use the pictures and the guide, or create a new conversation.**

A: Hello?

B: Hi, _____. This is _____. What are you doing?

A: I'm _____.

B: Should I call you back later?

A: Yes, thanks. Talk to you later. Bye.

B: _____.

3 ▶ *Discuss Plans*

THURSDAY
1. this morning
2. this afternoon
3. this evening
4. tonight

A 🎧 **VOCABULARY.** Time expressions.
Listen and practice.

SUNDAY	MONDAY	TUESDAY	WEDNESDAY	THURSDAY	FRIDAY	SATURDAY

5. today   6. tomorrow   7. the day after tomorrow

B **GRAMMAR.** The present continuous: continuing activities and future plans ───

Use the present continuous for actions that continue in the present.
I'm studying English **this year**.   I'm working at home **this week**.

Use the present continuous for future plans.
They're cleaning the house **on Friday**, not today.   Janet's meeting Bill **at 5:00**.

C **Read Beth Rand's date book for this week.**

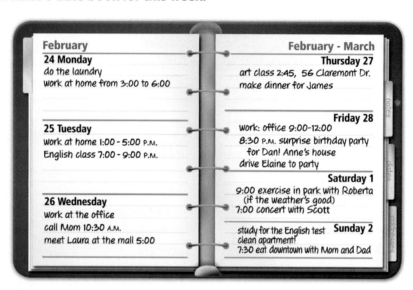

February
24 Monday
do the laundry
work at home from 3:00 to 6:00

25 Tuesday
work at home 1:00 – 5:00 P.M.
English class 7:00 – 9:00 P.M.

26 Wednesday
work at the office
call Mom 10:30 A.M.
meet Laura at the mall 5:00

February – March
Thursday 27
art class 2:45, 56 Claremont Dr.
make dinner for James

Friday 28
work: office 9:00–12:00
8:30 P.M. surprise birthday party
     for Dan! Anne's house
drive Elaine to party

Saturday 1
9:00 exercise in park with Roberta
     (if the weather's good)
7:00 concert with Scott

Sunday 2
study for the English test
clean apartment!
7:30 eat downtown with Mom and Dad

Now complete each statement with the present continuous. Use the affirmative and negative.

1. On Monday, Beth ___*is doing the laundry*___ and ___*working at home*___
   from 3:00 to 6:00.

2. On Tuesday, she _____ from 1:00 to 5:00.

3. The next day, Wednesday, she _____ Laura at the mall.

4. Thursday afternoon, she _____ at 2:45.

5. Later that day, she _____ for James.

6. On Friday, at 8:30, Beth _____ to Dan's party.

7. Beth _____ Elaine to the party.

8. On Saturday morning, Beth _____ in the park with Roberta.

9. In the evening, she _____ with Scott.

10. On Sunday, she _____ and _____.

11. On Sunday night, she _____ downtown with her parents.

CONVERSATION · *Discuss plans.*

1. 🎧 **MODEL.** **Read and listen.**

Scott: So what are you doing this weekend?

Dan: I'm not sure. What about you?

Scott: Well, on Saturday, if the weather is good, I'm meeting Pam in the park.

Dan: Do you want to get together on Sunday? I'm not doing anything special.

Scott: Sure. Call me Sunday morning.

2. 🎧 **Rhythm and intonation practice**

3. **WHAT ABOUT YOU?** **Fill in the date book for this week. Write your activities and the times.**

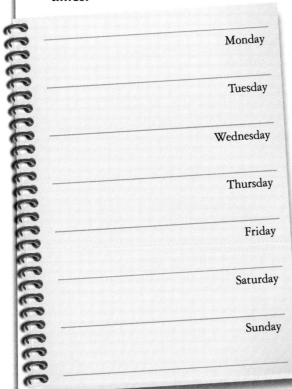

_____ Monday

_____ Tuesday

_____ Wednesday

_____ Thursday

_____ Friday

_____ Saturday

_____ Sunday

4. **PAIR WORK.** **Now make plans with your partner. Use your date book. Use this guide, or create a new conversation.**

A: So what are you doing _____?

B: _____. What about you?

A: Well, _____.

B: Do you want to get together _____? I'm not doing anything special.

A: _____. Call me _____.

TOP NOTCH
ACTIVITIES

 A 🎧 **READING.** Read and listen to the instant messages.

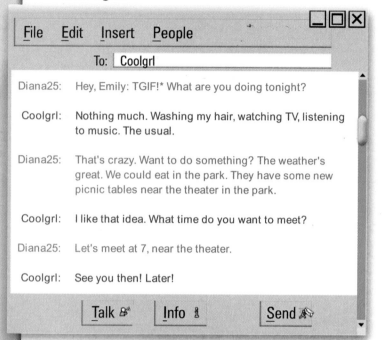

File   Edit   Insert   People

To: Coolgrl

Diana25:	Hey, Emily: TGIF!* What are you doing tonight?
Coolgrl:	Nothing much. Washing my hair, watching TV, listening to music. The usual.
Diana25:	That's crazy. Want to do something? The weather's great. We could eat in the park. They have some new picnic tables near the theater in the park.
Coolgrl:	I like that idea. What time do you want to meet?
Diana25:	Let's meet at 7, near the theater.
Coolgrl:	See you then! Later!

Talk 🐿   Info ⓘ   Send 📨

*T-G-I-F = Thank goodness it's Friday.

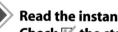 **B** Read the instant messages again. Check ☑ the statements that are true.

1. ☐ It's Friday.
2. ☐ Emily's not planning anything special.
3. ☐ It's not raining.
4. ☐ They're meeting at 7:00.
5. ☐ They're going to a play in the park.
6. ☐ They're eating lunch in the park.

 C **GROUP WORK.** Walk around the class. Make plans to meet three classmates.

❝ What are you doing on Saturday? ❞

❝ I'm not doing anything special. Do you want to go to a movie? ❞

NEED HELP? Here's language you already know:

Events and places
a play   a party
a movie   a game
a concert   a speech

at the [stadium]
on the corner of [First Street]
    and [Main Street]
next to the [school]

Times and dates
on [Monday]
this weekend
in the evening
at [eight] o'clock

Questions
Would you like to go?
Do you want to get together?
Let's meet at [two thirty].

Weather expressions
It's [hot].
The weather is [beautiful].

 D **WRITING.** On a separate piece of paper, write your plans for the next three days.

 TOP NOTCH WEBSITE
For Unit 9 online activities, visit the *Top Notch* Companion Website at www.longman.com/topnotch.

UNIT WRAP-UP

- **Grammar.** Talk about the pictures. Use the present continuous.
  They're going to a concert. She's talking on the phone.

- **Social language.** Create conversations for the people.
  A: Let's meet later.
  B: OK. What time?

Thursday
6:30 P.M.

Concert

6:30 P.M.
Tonight

Saturday
9:00 A.M.

✓ *Now I can...*

☐ describe today's weather.
☐ ask about people's activities.
☐ discuss plans.

83

Food

UNIT GOALS

1 Get ingredients for a recipe
2 Offer and ask for foods at the table
3 Talk about present-time activities

LESSON 1

Get Ingredients for a Recipe

A 🎧 **VOCABULARY.** Foods: count nouns. **Listen and practice.**

1. an egg
2. an onion
3. an apple
4. an orange
5. a lemon
6. a banana
7. a tomato
8. a potato
9. a pepper
10. beans
11. peas

📖 **VOCABULARY BOOSTER** See pages V6 and V7 for more.

B 🎧 **LISTENING COMPREHENSION.** Listen to the conversations. Check ☑ the foods from the vocabulary you hear in each conversation. Then listen again to check your work.

1.		✔			✔		
2.							
3.							
4.							
5.							

C **GRAMMAR.** How many and Are there any

Use How many and Are there any with plural nouns.

How many tomatoes are there?	Two.
How many peppers are there in the fridge?	Four.
Are there any lemons in the fridge?	Yes. There are three. / No, there aren't [any].

D 🎧 **VOCABULARY.** Places to keep food in a kitchen. **Listen and practice.**

1. in the fridge (*or* in the refrigerator)   2. on the shelf   3. on the counter

E **PAIR WORK.** **Ask your partner questions about the pictures in Exercise D. Use <u>How many</u> and <u>Are there any</u>. Answer your partner's questions.**

❝ Are there any beans in the fridge? ❞

❝ No, there aren't any. ❞

CONVERSATION • *Get ingredients for a recipe.*

1. 🎧 **MODEL.** **Read and listen.**

Wendy: How about some tomato potato soup?

Fred: Tomato potato? That sounds delicious! I love tomatoes and potatoes.

Wendy: Are there any potatoes on the shelf?

Fred: Yes, there are.

Wendy: And do we have any tomatoes?

Fred: I'll check.

2. 🎧 **Rhythm and intonation practice**

3. **PAIR WORK.** **Role-play a conversation. Use the recipes. Start like this:**

A: How about some _____?

B: _____? That sounds delicious! I love _____.

A: Are there any _____?

B: _____ . . .

Continue in your <u>own</u> way . . .

Tomato Potato Soup
Ingredients:
tomatoes
potatoes
onions

Fruit Salad
Ingredients:
apples
bananas
oranges

Green Bean Salad
Ingredients:
beans
peas
onions

Potato Pancakes
Ingredients:
potatoes
onions
eggs

Stuffed Peppers
Ingredients:
peppers
tomatoes
onions

Offer and Ask for Foods at the Table

 VOCABULARY. Drinks and foods: non-count nouns. Listen and practice.

Drinks

1. water   2. coffee   3. tea   4. juice   5. milk   6. soda

Foods

7. bread   8. pasta   9. rice   10. cheese   11. meat   12. chicken

13. fish   14. oil   15. butter   16. sugar   17. salt   18. pepper

 GRAMMAR. Non-count nouns

"Count nouns" name things you can count. They can be singular or plural.

I want an apple.
I like bananas.
We have three tomatoes.

"Non-count nouns" name things you can not count. They are not singular or plural.

I don't eat sugar. NOT a sugar and NOT sugars

Be careful! Always use singular verbs with non-count nouns.

Rice is good for you. NOT Rice are good for you.

 Complete the chart with things you eat and drink. Use count and non-count nouns.

I eat	
I don't eat	
I drink	
I don't drink	

86 UNIT 10

GRAMMAR. <u>How much</u> and <u>Is there any</u>

Use <u>How much</u> and <u>Is there any</u> with non-count nouns.
How much sugar do you want?
Is there any milk in the fridge?

But remember: Use <u>How many</u> and <u>Are there any</u> with plural count nouns.
How many apples are there in the kitchen?
Are there any bananas?

 VOCABULARY. Containers and quantities.
Listen and practice.

1. a box of pasta   **2. a loaf** of bread   **3. a bottle** of juice   **4. a can** of soup   **5. a bag** of onions

F Complete each question with <u>How much</u> or <u>How many</u>.

1. <u>How many</u> boxes of pasta are there in the kitchen?

2. _____ eggs are there in the fridge?

3. _____ rice is there on the shelf?

4. _____ bottles of juice are there on the shelf?

5. _____ sugar is in that coffee?

6. _____ cans of tomatoes do we have?

CONVERSATION • *Offer and ask for foods at the table.*

1. **MODEL.** **Read and listen.**

Linda: Would you like coffee or tea?
Nicole: I'd like coffee, please. Thanks.
Linda: And would you like sugar?
Nicole: No, thanks.
Linda: Please pass the butter.
Nicole: Sure. Here you go.

2. **Rhythm and intonation practice**

3. **PAIR WORK.** Role-play a conversation at the table. Use the guide, or create a new conversation.

A: Would you like _____ or _____?
B: I'd like _____, please. _____.
A: And would you like _____?
B: _____. . .

Continue in your <u>own</u> way . . .

3 Talk about Present-time Activities

A ▶ **GRAMMAR.** The present continuous and the simple present tense

Use the present continuous for actions that continue in the present.
He's **eating** dinner now.
We're **studying** English this year.

Use the simple present tense for habitual actions.
My husband **cooks** dinner for our family.
I never **eat** eggs for breakfast. NOT I ~~am never eating~~ eggs for breakfast.

Use the simple present tense with **want**, **need**, and **like**.
I **like** coffee. NOT I ~~am liking~~ coffee.

B ▶ Complete each statement or question with the simple present tense or the present continuous.

1. Who _____ lunch today?
   make

2. We _____ any sugar.
   not need

3. She sometimes _____ lunch early.
   eat

4. They _____ milk in their coffee.
   not like

5. I _____ the kitchen every day.
   clean

6. I'm busy. I _____ the kids.
   feed

7. What _____?
   Peter / need

8. _____ onion soup?
   you / like

9. What _____ now?
   they / do

10. How much sugar _____ in your tea?
    you / want

C ▶ **WRITING.** Look at the picture of Louisa Brown and her date book. On a separate piece of paper, write about Louisa. What is she doing right now? What does she do at other times? Use the present continuous and the simple present tense.

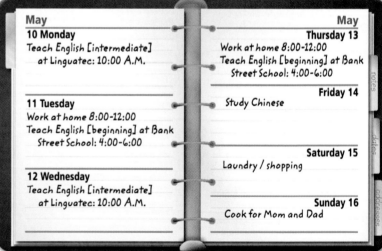

Louisa is listening to music right now. On Mondays
and Wednesdays, she teaches English at Linguatec.

D ▶ **PAIR WORK.** Write <u>yes</u> / <u>no</u> and information questions about Louisa. Use the present continuous and the simple present tense.

88   UNIT 10

PRONUNCIATION. Vowel sounds. **Listen and practice.**

1. /i/	2. /ɪ/	3. /eɪ/	4. /ɛ/	5. /æ/
see	six	late	pepper	apple
tea	fish	potato	said	balcony
street	big	train	lemon	factory

CONVERSATION • *Invite someone to join you.*

1. **MODEL.** **Read and listen.**

Rita: Hey, Alison. Would you like to join me?

Alison: Sure. What are you drinking?

Rita: Lemonade.

Alison: Mmm. Sounds great. I think I'd like the same thing.

2. **Rhythm and intonation practice**

3. **PAIR WORK.** **Role-play a conversation. Use the guide, or create a new conversation.**

A: Hey, _____. Would you like to join me?

B: Sure. What are you _____?

A: _____.

B: Mmm. Sounds great. I think I'd like _____ . . .

Continue in your <u>own</u> way . . .

TOP NOTCH
ACTIVITIES

TOP NOTCH WEBSITE
For Unit 10 online activities, visit the *Top Notch* Companion Website at www.longman.com/topnotch.

A 🎧 **READING.** Read and listen to the two recipes.

Garlic and Oil Spaghetti

Ingredients
4 medium cloves of garlic
6 tablespoons of olive oil
8 ounces (500 grams) of spaghetti

1. Boil a large pot of water.
2. Cook the spaghetti.
3. Drain the spaghetti.
4. Chop the garlic.
5. Saute the garlic in the olive oil until it is yellow / brown—not too dark!
6. Mix the garlic, cooked spaghetti, and 1/3 cup of the cooking water in a bowl.
7. Serve with salt and pepper.

Hungarian Cabbage and Noodles

Ingredients
1 large head of green cabbage
1/2 cup unsalted butter
11 ounces (700 grams) of egg noodles

1. Slice the cabbage into thin slices.
2. Put the cabbage into a large bowl and sprinkle with salt.
3. Put the cabbage into the refrigerator overnight.
4. The next day, drain the cabbage.
5. Melt the butter in a large pan. Saute the cabbage until it is light brown and very soft (30–40 minutes).
6. Cook the noodles.
7. Drain the noodles and mix them with the cabbage.
8. Add lots of black pepper.

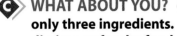

Source: Adapted from *Recipes 1-2-3* by Rozanne Gold (New York: Viking, 1997)

B Answer the questions.

1. Are there any onions in the recipes? _____
2. Is there any pasta in the recipes? _____
3. Which recipe has butter? _____
4. Which recipe has garlic? _____

C **WHAT ABOUT YOU?** **Create your <u>own</u> recipe with only three ingredients. Write the ingredients. Use a dictionary for the food names you don't know. Then tell the class about your recipe.**

> ❝ My recipe is for my grandmother's chicken soup. It's very good… ❞

Name of food: _____
Ingredients:
_____
_____
_____

UNIT WRAP-UP

- **Vocabulary.** Look at the picture. Close your book. Write the names of all the foods and drinks you remember.

- **Grammar.** Ask questions about the picture. Use <u>How much</u>, <u>How many</u>, <u>Is there any</u>, and <u>Are there any</u>.
  A: How much pasta is there?   B: Four boxes.

- **Writing.** Write sentences about what the people are doing and their schedules.
  Michelle cleans the apartment on Mondays.

- **Social language.** Create conversations for Michelle and Peter.
  A: How about some potato pancakes?
  B: That sounds delicious.

TUESDAY

Monday/Wednesday/Friday
  clean apartment—Michelle
  cook—Peter
Tuesday/Thursday/Sunday
  shop, do laundry—Peter
  cook—Michelle
Saturday—NO CHORES!

Milk

Pasta Pasta Tea
Pasta Pasta

Shopping List
onions
potatoes
tomatoes
apples
rice
coffee
milk
bread
soda
juice
lemons

Potato Pancakes
Ingredients:
2 large potatoes
1 small onion
Oil
2 eggs

LATER

SATURDAY

✓	**Now I can ...**
☐	get ingredients for a recipe.
☐	offer and ask for foods at the table.
☐	talk about present-time activities.

91

UNIT 11

Past Events

UNIT GOALS

1 Talk about the past
2 Discuss past activities
3 Ask about a vacation

Talk about the Past

A 🎧 **VOCABULARY.** Past-time expressions. **Listen and practice.**

4. nineteen ninety-eight   5. two thousand

🎧 **How to say years**

1900 = nineteen hundred
1901 = nineteen oh one
2001 = two thousand and one
2010 = two thousand ten
1980–1989 = the (nineteen) eighties
1901–2000 = the twentieth century
2001–3000 = the twenty-first century

B 🎧 **LISTENING COMPREHENSION.** Listen to the years. Point to the year you hear.

C **PAIR WORK.** Now choose five years from the chart. Say a year to your partner. Your partner circles the year.

2007	1907	1812
1940	1914	1900
1705	2017	1905
1805	1999	1919
2006	1814	1800

D **GRAMMAR.** The past tense of be

I
He ⎫ **was** at home last night.
She ⎭

We
You ⎫ **were** colleagues in 1995.
They ⎭

It **was** cloudy yesterday.
She **wasn't** at work last Monday.

There **were** a lot of people in the park this morning.
We **weren't** at the party last night.

Contractions
was not → **wasn't**
were not → **weren't**

Was Richard at school yesterday?
Where was his brother last night?
When was she in France?

Were your parents students in 1985?
Where were they two days ago?
When were you sick?

E Complete the sentences. Write <u>was</u> or <u>were</u>.

1. _____ she a student in 1995?
2. What _____ their address last year?
3. Where _____ Peter and Jen last week?
4. _____ there a party last night?
5. My parents _____ students in the seventies.
6. _____ his brothers at the park yesterday?
7. There _____ a lot of closets in her first house.
8. When _____ your father in Thailand?

F 🎧 LISTENING COMPREHENSION. **Listen to the conversations about events. Then listen again and circle the day or month.**

1. If today is Saturday, the party was on (Saturday / Friday / Thursday).
2. If this is May, then her birthday was in (June / April / March).
3. If today is Wednesday, the game was on (Monday / Tuesday / Sunday).

CONVERSATION • *Talk about the past.*

1. 🎧 MODEL. **Read and listen.**

Terri: Where were you last night?

Ruth: When?

Terri: At about 8:00.

Ruth: I was at home. Why?

Terri: There was a great party at the Pike Museum.

Ruth: There was? Too bad I wasn't there!

2. 🎧 **Rhythm and intonation practice**

3. PAIR WORK. **Now role-play the conversation. Use the pictures and the guide, or create a new conversation.**

A: Where were you _____?

B: When?

A: At _____.

B: I was _____. Why?

A: There was _____ at _____.

B: _____.

at the Drama School

at Smith Stadium

at Brown Park

2 Discuss Past Activities

A GRAMMAR. The simple past tense

Regular verbs

Add -ed to form the simple past tense. If the verb ends in -e, just add -d.

call → called   like → liked

I called my mother yesterday, but she wasn't home.

> **But remember:**
> study → studied
> shop → shopped

Irregular verbs

🎧 **Learn these irregular past tense forms.**

come → came	have → had	take → took
do → did	make → made	wake → woke
drive → drove	put → put	wear → wore
eat → ate	read → read	write → wrote
get → got	ride → rode	
go → went	see → saw	

To make negative statements, use didn't (did not) and the base form of a verb.

I didn't go to the movies last night. NOT I ~~didn't went~~ to the movies last night.

B 🎧 PRONUNCIATION. The simple past tense ending. Listen and practice.

1. /d/
played = play/d/
listened = listen/d/
exercised = exercise/d/

2. /t/
liked = like/t/
washed = wash/t/
shopped = shop/t/

3. /ɪd/
wanted = want/ɪd/
needed = need/ɪd/

C Complete the postcard with the simple past tense form of the verbs.

Dear Sally,
Greetings from San Francisco. I _____ a great
time yesterday. In the morning, I _____ to the
1. have   **2.** go
Museum of Modern Art. It _____ really great,
3. be
and I _____ the art a lot. For lunch, I _____ at
4. like   **5.** eat
a nice Italian restaurant called Little City. In the
afternoon, I _____ the cable car to Ghirardelli
6. take
Square. I _____ them make chocolate there.
7. watch
I _____ all over Fisherman's Wharf, and I
8. walk
_____ a lot of interesting people.
9. see

Thinking of you!
George

a cable car

Ghirardelli Chocolate

D WRITING. On a separate piece of paper, write three things you did yesterday. Write three things you didn't do. Then tell your partner about your day.

> "I made dinner last night. But I didn't wash the dishes."

Fisherman's Wharf

E 🎧 **VOCABULARY.** Weekend activities.
Listen and practice.

1. go to the beach

2. go running

3. go bike riding

4. go for a walk

5. go swimming

6. go for a drive

📖 **VOCABULARY BOOSTER** See page V7 for more.

CONVERSATION • *Discuss past activities.*

1. 🎧 **MODEL. Read and listen.**

Hugo: Hi, Saul. How's it going?

Saul: Pretty good, thanks.

Hugo: What did you do last weekend?

Saul: Not much. I went running in the park on Saturday. What about you?

Hugo: About the same. I played soccer and went to a movie.

2. 🎧 **Rhythm and intonation practice**

3. PAIR WORK. Now exchange real information or use the pictures.

A: Hi, _____. How's it going?

B: _____.

A: What did you do _____?

B: Not much. I _____. What about you?

A: _____ . . .

Continue in your <u>own</u> way . . .

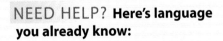

NEED HELP? **Here's language you already know:**

Past-time expressions
last week
last weekend
last month
last Friday

3 *Ask about a Vacation*

A 🎧 VOCABULARY. Seasons. Listen and practice.

1. spring

2. summer

3. fall / autumn

4. winter

B DISCUSSION. Tell a classmate your favorite season. What do you do during that season?

> 〝 My favorite season is summer.
> It's hot. I go swimming. 〞

C GRAMMAR. The simple past tense: questions

To ask questions about the past, use <u>did</u> and the base form of a verb.

<u>Yes</u> / <u>no</u> questions

Did { I / you / he / she / we / they } **watch** TV last night?

Short answers

Yes, { I / you / he / she } **did**.

No, { we / they } **didn't**.

Information questions

What did you do last summer?

Where did she go last winter?

Who did they see yesterday?

When did he come home last night?

How many eggs **did** you **eat** this morning?

How often did you **go** swimming last week?

D Complete the questions in the simple past tense.

1. **A:** _____ she _____ to the beach last summer?
   B: No, she went to her parents' house.

2. **A:** Where _____ they _____ dinner?
   B: They ate dinner at the Spring Street Cafe.

3. **A:** Who _____ she _____ last weekend?
   B: She saw her new classmate, Paul.

4. **A:** How often _____ he _____ bike riding?
   B: He went every day.

5. **A:** How many books _____ you _____?
   B: I read about three.

6. **A:** _____ you _____ the new restaurant?
   B: Yes, I really liked it.

PAIR WORK. **Ask your partner questions about past activities.**

" Did you exercise last weekend? "

CONVERSATION • *Ask about a vacation.*

1. 🎧 **MODEL.** **Read and listen.**

Brian: You look great. Were you on vacation?

Naomi: Yes, I was. I just got back last week.

Brian: Where did you go?

Naomi: I went to London for two weeks.

Brian: No kidding. How was it?

Naomi: Really nice.

Brian: Well, it's great to see you. Welcome back.

Naomi: Thanks.

2. 🎧 **Rhythm and intonation practice**

3. **PAIR WORK.** **Choose a vacation place. Use the photos or another place. Then role-play the conversation.**

A: You look ____. Were you on vacation?

B: ____. I just got back ____.

A: Where did you go?

B: ____.

A: ____. How was it?

B: ____ . . .

Continue in your own way . . .

🎧 **Positive and negative descriptions**

☺
Really nice.
Great.
Wonderful.

☹
Not good.
Terrible.
Awful.

Rio de Janeiro

Moscow

Rome

London

Hawaii

Istanbul

Hong Kong

World's Top 10 Tourism Destinations
1 France   6 United Kingdom
2 Spain   7 Russian Federation
3 United States 8 Mexico
4 Italy   9 Canada
5 China   10 Austria

Source: World Tourism Organization (WTO)©

A ⌂ **READING.** **Read and listen.** **What's your dream vacation?**

Where Did You Go on Vacation?

Luz Rodriguez

Last summer, my husband and I went to Paris for the first time. It was wonderful — we did so many things. Every night, we listened to music and went to bed late. And every morning, we got up late.

During the day, we walked the streets and visited tourist sites like the Eiffel Tower and the Louvre. We sat in cafes, drank coffee, and watched people. The food was great — we ate too much. I loved the bread and the cheese.

sunset in Cancun

snorkeling

Tulum

a Paris cafe

the Louvre   *the Eiffel Tower*

Yoko Mia Hirano

Two years ago, my friends and I spent two weeks in Cancun, Mexico. We had a fantastic time. The beaches were just beautiful! The water was so blue and warm.

Every morning we watched the sunrise, and in the evening we ate dinner on the beach and watched the sunset. The food was really good — the fish and fruit juices were very fresh. We went swimming right next to the ruins at Tulum. We took a water taxi to Isla Mujeres and went snorkeling. We saw so many beautiful fish!

John Barnes

My wife and I went to Hong Kong in 2003. What a great city! Every day, we went sightseeing. We took the ferry to Kowloon and looked at the beautiful views of the city. We went to Aberdeen and ate dinner on a boat. We visited the Tiger Balm Garden.

We mainly ate Chinese food, but sometimes we had Thai food or French food. The food in Hong Kong is terrific! My favorite was a dim sum restaurant that can serve 4800 people.

a Hong Kong ferry

dim sum

Source: Authentic *Top Notch* interviews

B **Answer the questions.** **Write sentences on a separate piece of paper.**

1. Who went on vacation with her friends?
2. What did Luz Rodriguez do at night?
3. Who ate dinner on a boat?
4. What foods did Luz Rodriguez like?
5. How did John Barnes get to Kowloon?
6. What did Yoko Mia Hirano do in the evening?

C **DISCUSSION.** **Where do you want to go on vacation?**

 " Me? I really want to go to Austria. "

D **WRITING.** **On a separate piece of paper, write about a vacation that you took. Where did you go? What did you do? Then tell your class about your vacation.**

 I went to the beach last summer. Every day I . . .

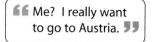 ⌂ **TOP NOTCH SONG**
"My Favorite Day"
Lyrics on last page before Workbook.

 TOP NOTCH WEBSITE
For Unit 11 online activities, visit the *Top Notch* Companion Website at
www.longman.com/topnotch.

UNIT WRAP-UP

- **Social language.** Create conversations for Don Baker and Karen Taylor. Ask about last weekend. Ask about a vacation.
  A: What did you do last weekend?
  B: Not much. On Saturday I went shopping.

- **Writing.** Choose Don or Karen. Write about what he or she did.
  Last Saturday Karen went shopping . . .

Last Saturday

Last Weekend

Last Vacation

Last Vacation

✓ **Now I can . . .**

- ☐ talk about the past.
- ☐ discuss past activities.
- ☐ ask about a vacation.

99

UNIT **12**

Appearance and Health

UNIT GOALS

1 Describe people
2 Show concern about an injury
3 Suggest a remedy

Describe People

A 🎧 **VOCABULARY.** Adjectives to describe hair. **Listen and practice.**

1. black   2. brown   3. red    4. blonde   5. gray    6. white

14. a mustache
15. a beard

7. dark ⟵   ⟶ 8. light

 9. straight   10. wavy   11. curly   12. short   13. long

16. bald

B 🎧 **LISTENING COMPREHENSION.**
Listen to the descriptions of hair.
Write the number next to the picture.

C 🎧 **VOCABULARY.** The face.
Listen and practice.

 ①

8. brown eyes

9. blue eyes

10. green eyes

11. eyelashes

1. eye
2. eyebrow

4. ear

3. nose

5. mouth

7. neck

12. tooth
13. tongue

6. chin

one tooth → two **teeth**

D GRAMMAR. Use of adjectives for physical description

With **be**		With **have**
My eyes are blue.	OR	I have blue eyes.
Our hair is blonde.	OR	We have blonde hair.
Her eyelashes are long and dark.	OR	She has long, dark eyelashes.

E Complete the sentences with a form of **be** or **have**.

1. My sister's hair _____ long and wavy.

2. Paul's brother _____ curly, black hair.

3. My grandfather _____ a short, gray beard.

4. Her eyes _____ very beautiful.

5. Your sister's hair _____ so long!

6. We _____ straight, black hair.

CONVERSATION • *Describe people.*

1. ∩ MODEL. Read and listen.

Max: Who's that? She looks familiar.

Diane: Who?

Max: The woman with long, curly, blonde hair.

Diane: Oh, that's Daniela Mercury. She's a singer from Brazil.

Max: No kidding!

Daniela Mercury
singer (Brazil)

2. ∩ Rhythm and intonation practice

3. PAIR WORK. Now talk about the people in the photos.

A: Who's that? _____ looks familiar.

B: Who?

A: The _____ with _____.

B: Oh, that's _____. _____'s _____ from _____.

A: No kidding!

Andrea Boccelli
singer (Italy)

Chow Yun Fat
actor (Hong Kong)

Yao Ming
athlete (China)

Juliette Binoche
actress (France)

Luis Miguel
singer (Mexico)

101

Show Concern about an Injury

A 🎧 **VOCABULARY.** Parts of the body. **Listen and practice.**

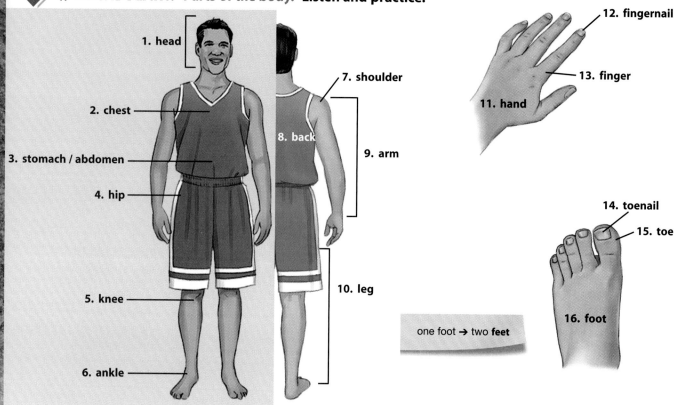

1. head
2. chest
3. stomach / abdomen
4. hip
5. knee
6. ankle
7. shoulder
8. back
9. arm
10. leg

11. hand
12. fingernail
13. finger

14. toenail
15. toe
16. foot

one foot → two **feet**

📖 **VOCABULARY BOOSTER** See page V8 for more.

B **GAME.** Practice the vocabulary. Follow a classmate's directions. If you make a mistake, sit down.

Touch your toes.

🎧 Base form		Past form
burn	→	burned
hurt	→	hurt
cut	→	cut
break	→	broke
fall	→	fell

C 🎧 **VOCABULARY.** Accidents and Injuries. **Listen and practice.**

1. He **burned** his finger.
2. She **hurt** her back.
3. She **cut** her hand.
4. He **broke** his arm.
5. He **fell down**.

⌒ **LISTENING COMPREHENSION. Listen. Write each injury. Then listen again to check your work.**

1. She ___burned her arm___ .

2. He _____ .

3. She _____ .

4. He _____ .

5. She _____ .

CONVERSATION • *Show concern about an injury.*

1. ⌒ **MODEL. Read and listen.**

Kate: Hey, Evan. What happened?

Evan: I broke my ankle.

Kate: I'm sorry to hear that.

2. ⌒ **Rhythm and intonation practice**

3. PAIR WORK. Now role-play the conversation. Use the pictures for ideas.

A: Hey, _____. What happened?

B: I _____.

A: I'm sorry to hear that.

103

3 Suggest a Remedy

A 🎧 VOCABULARY. Ailments. Listen and practice.

1. a headache

2. a stomachache

3. an earache

4. a backache

5. a toothache

6. a cold

7. a sore throat

8. a fever

9. a cough

10. a runny nose

B 🎧 LISTENING COMPREHENSION. Listen to the conversations. Check ☑ the ailments.

	a cold	a fever	a sore throat	a cough	a runny nose	a headache	a stomachache	a backache	a toothache
1.	☐	☐	☐	☐	☐	☐	☐	☐	☐
2.	☐	☐	☐	☐	☐	☐	☐	☐	☐
3.	☐	☐	☐	☐	☐	☐	☐	☐	☐
4.	☐	☐	☐	☐	☐	☐	☐	☐	☐
5.	☐	☐	☐	☐	☐	☐	☐	☐	☐
6.	☐	☐	☐	☐	☐	☐	☐	☐	☐

C 🎧 VOCABULARY. Remedies. Listen and practice.

1. take something

2. lie down

3. have some tea

4. see a doctor / dentist

D 🎧 PRONUNCIATION. Back-vowel sounds. Listen and practice.

1. /u/	**2.** /ʊ/	**3.** /oʊ/	**4.** /ɔ/	**5.** /ɑ/
tooth	foot	nose	cough	blonde
blue	good	toe	awful	hot
June	look	cold	daughter	doctor

E **GRAMMAR.** Should for advice

Ask for and give advice with should or shouldn't and the base form of a verb.

Questions
Should I see a doctor?
Should she take something?
What should she do?

Answers
Yes, you should.
No, she shouldn't.
She should go to bed.

I have a bad headache.

You should take something.

He has a fever.

He shouldn't go to school today.

F Suggest a remedy. Use should or shouldn't and the base form of a verb.

1. "I have a terrible backache."
   YOU _You should lie down_.

2. "I don't feel so good. I think I have a fever."
   YOU _____.

3. "Oh, my mouth! What a toothache!"
   YOU _____.

4. "My mother has a bad cough."
   YOU _____.

5. "My son has a stomachache. He feels awful!"
   YOU _____.

6. "I feel terrible. I have a sore throat."
   YOU _____.

CONVERSATION • *Suggest a remedy.*

1. 🎧 **MODEL. Read and listen.**

Bill: I feel awful.
Sally: What's wrong?
Bill: I have a headache.
Sally: You really should take something.
Bill: Good idea.
Sally: I hope you feel better.

2. 🎧 **Rhythm and intonation practice**

3. PAIR WORK. Choose an ailment. Role-play suggesting a remedy for your partner.
Use the guide, or create a new conversation.

B: I feel _____.
A: What's wrong?
B: _____.
A: You really _____.
B: _____.
A: I hope you feel better.

NEED HELP? **Here's language you already know:**

awful
terrible
bad

Good idea.
Thanks.
OK.

105

TOP NOTCH
ACTIVITIES

A 🎧 **READING.** Look at the photos. Read and listen. Write the name of each person.

Gerard Depardieu
actor

Zhang Zi Yi
actress

Caetano Veloso
singer

Rob Reiner
film director

Julia Roberts
actress

1. She's very pretty. She has straight, black hair and brown eyes. She's wearing a red dress.
   name _____

2. He's wearing a white shirt and a black jacket. He has brownish-blonde hair and blue eyes.
   name _____

3. He has blue eyes and a gray beard. His eyebrows are brown. He's bald. He's wearing a tie and a blue shirt.
   name _____

4. He's handsome and has wavy, black hair. His eyes are brown. He's wearing a blue shirt.
   name _____

5. She has long, red hair. She has pretty, brown eyes. She's wearing a black dress.
   name _____

B **GUESSING GAME.** On a separate piece of paper, write a description of a classmate. Read your description to the class. The class guesses who it is.

She's short and very good-looking. She has long hair and brown eyes. She's wearing a white blouse and a blue skirt.

TOP NOTCH WEBSITE
For Unit 12 online activities, visit the *Top Notch* Companion Website at www.longman.com/topnotch.

UNIT WRAP-UP

- **Vocabulary.** Make statements about the ailments and injuries in the picture.
  She has a cold.

- **Grammar.** Suggest remedies for the people in the picture.
  She should take something.

- **Social language.** Create conversations for the people.
  A: What happened?
  B: I fell down.

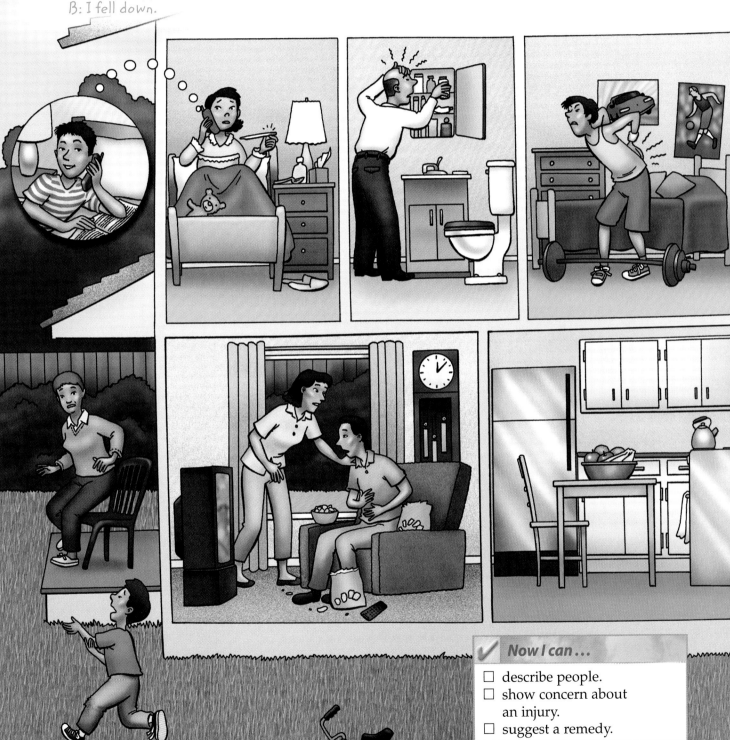

✓ Now I can...

- ☐ describe people.
- ☐ show concern about an injury.
- ☐ suggest a remedy.

UNIT 13

Abilities and Requests

UNIT GOALS

1 Discuss abilities
2 Decline an invitation
3 Request help or permission

1 ▶ Discuss Abilities

Ⓐ GRAMMAR. Can and can't

To talk about ability, use can or can't and the base form of a verb.

Questions
Can you **play** the guitar?
Can he **speak** English?

Short answers
Yes, I **can**. / No, I **can't**.
Yes, he **can**. / No, he **can't**.

can not → cannot → can't

She **can play** the guitar.   He **can't cook**.

Ⓑ **PRONUNCIATION.** Can and can't. **Notice the pronunciation _and_ stress. Listen and practice.**

/kən/   /kænt/

1. I can play the guitar.   I can't play the piano.

2. I can speak English.   I can't speak Italian.

3. I can make pasta.   I can't make soup.

Ⓒ **VOCABULARY.** Abilities and skills. **Listen and practice.**

1. sew   2. knit   3. paint   4. draw   5. dance

6. swim   7. drive   8. play the violin   9. ski   10. fix a car

📖 **VOCABULARY BOOSTER** See page V8 for more.

Ⓓ Check ☑ **the things _you_ can do. Then tell your class about yourself.**

" I can't play the guitar, but I can sing. "

I can:	☐ sew	☐ drive	☐ fix a car	☐ ski
	☐ knit	☐ sing	☐ paint	☐ cook
	☐ dance	☐ play the guitar	☐ draw	☐ swim

E 🎧 **VOCABULARY.** Adverbs to describe ability. **Listen and practice.**

1. Tom sings { **well.**
                beautifully.
                nicely.

2. Ryan sings { **badly.**
                 poorly.
                 terribly.

> **Be careful!**
> He speaks English well.
> NOT ~~He speaks well English.~~

F Complete the conversations with **can** or **can't** and the base form of a verb.

1. **A:** _____ you _____ a car?
   B: Yes, I _____. But I don't drive well.

2. **A:** _____ John _____ well?
   B: Yes, he _____. He swims nicely.

3. **A:** _____ your brother _____?
   B: No. He _____ cook at all.

4. **A:** _____ Gloria _____ English well?
   B: Yes. She speaks English well.

5. **A:** _____ your grandmother _____?
   B: Yes. She knits beautifully.

6. **A:** _____ you _____ the guitar?
   B: No, I _____. I play very badly.

CONVERSATION • *Discuss abilities.*

1. 🎧 **MODEL.** **Read and listen.**

Gene: Can you swim?
Amy: No. Can you?
Gene: Yes. I swim very well.
Amy: When did you learn?
Gene: When I was about eight.
Amy: Was it hard?
Gene: Not at all!

2. 🎧 **Rhythm and intonation practice**

3. PAIR WORK. **Now exchange real information.**

A: Can you _____?
B: _____. Can you?
A: _____ . . .

Continue in your <u>own</u> way . . .

2 ▶ *Decline an Invitation*

Ⓐ GRAMMAR. <u>Too</u> + adjective ──────────────

Use <u>too</u> with an adjective to express a problem.

I can't drink this tea.
It's **too hot**.

I don't want those shoes.
They're **too expensive**.

I can't read.
I'm **too tired**.

Ⓑ Write sentences with <u>too</u> and an adjective.

1. I can't eat this soup.

   It's too hot .

4. She can't wear those pants.

   _____ .

2. She can't buy those shoes.

   _____ .

5. He doesn't want that shirt.

   _____ .

3. I don't want this sofa.

   _____ .

6. She can't go swimming today.

   _____ .

C 🎧 **VOCABULARY.** Reasons to decline an invitation. **Listen and practice.**

1. **I'm too busy.**

2. **I don't feel well.**

3. **It's too late.**

4. **I have other plans.**

CONVERSATION • *Decline an invitation.*

1. 🎧 **MODEL. Read and listen.**

Carl: Let's go to the movies.

Lucy: I'm really sorry. I'm too busy.

Carl: That's too bad. Maybe some other time.

2. 🎧 **Rhythm and intonation practice**

3. **PAIR WORK. Suggest an activity. Decline the invitation. Use the photos or other places and events.**

A: Let's _____.

B: I'm really sorry. _____.

A: _____. Maybe some other time.

Request Help or Permission

A 🎧 **VOCABULARY.** <u>Could you please . . . ?</u> **Listen and practice.**

1. Could you please open the window?

2. Could you please close the door?

3. Could you please turn on the light?

4. Could you please turn off the TV?

5. Could you please help me?

6. Could you please hand me my glasses?

B 🎧 **LISTENING COMPREHENSION.** **Listen to the requests. Write the number on the correct picture. Then listen again to check your work.**

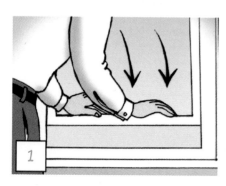

1

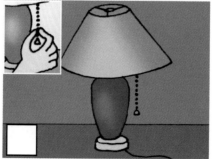

GRAMMAR. Requests with <u>Could</u> or <u>Can</u>

Use questions with <u>Could you</u> or <u>Can you</u> and the base form of a verb to make requests.

Could you turn on the light? OR **Can you** turn on the light?

Use <u>please</u> to make a request more polite.

Could you **please** help me? OR Can you **please** help me?

Use questions with <u>can</u> or <u>could</u> and the base form to ask for permission.

Can I please open the window?   Sure. No problem.
Could we watch TV?   No, not now. Sorry.

D Complete the polite requests for help or permission. Use <u>please</u>.

1. After dinner, *could you please wash* the dishes?

2. I'm so cold. _____ the window?

3. _____ the laundry this afternoon?

4. _____ the garbage tonight?

5. It's so windy. _____ the door?

6. _____ lunch? I'm too busy!

CONVERSATION • *Request help.*

1. 🎧 **MODEL. Read and listen.**

Tina: Could you do me a favor?

Roger: Sure. What?

Tina: Could you please close the window?

Roger: No problem.

2. 🎧 **Rhythm and intonation practice**

3. PAIR WORK. Now ask your partner to do you a favor.

A: Could you do me a favor?

B: _____. What?

A: Could you please _____?

B: _____.

NEED HELP? Here's language you already know:

Possible responses
Sure. No problem.
Sorry, I can't. I'm too busy.

TOP NOTCH **WEBSITE**
For Unit 13 online activities, visit the
Top Notch Companion Website at
www.longman.com/topnotch.

A 🎧 **READING.** Read and listen.

From infant to toddler . . .

At birth, an infant needs his or her parents to do everything—the baby cannot do anything alone. But before the age of two, there is a lot of learning.

lying   sitting   crawling   walking

Between 1 and 3 months the baby can:	Between 3 and 6 months the baby can:	Between 6 and 12 months the baby can:	Between 1 and 2 years the baby can:

Between 1 and 3 months the baby can:

• turn her head or smile when her mother or father speaks

• roll over

• cry when she's hungry, thirsty, or afraid
• see colors

Between 3 and 6 months the baby can:

• sit with help

• see an object and reach for it
• look at his own hands and feet
• make an <u>m</u> sound
• laugh
• look when someone says his name
• push with his feet

Between 6 and 12 months the baby can:

• crawl and stand

• pick up small objects
• say a few words
• cry for attention
• sit without help
• eat crackers

Between 1 and 2 years the baby can:

• feed herself

• throw objects
• say "no" and "mine"
• follow directions
• play next to other children
• walk
• sit down

Source: http://www.nncc.org

B Check ☑ the things that a five-month-old baby can do, according to the article.

☐ smile   ☐ feed itself   ☐ say a few words
☐ see colors   ☐ laugh   ☐ roll over
☐ walk   ☐ sit without help   ☐ reach for an object
☐ crawl and stand   ☐ pick up small objects   ☐ throw objects

C Complete the sentences about what a baby **can't** do.

1. At two months, <u>a baby can't walk</u> .

2. At two months, _____ .

3. At four months, _____ .

4. At eight months, _____ .

D **DISCUSSION.** Discuss things children can and can't do at other ages.

UNIT WRAP-UP

- **Vocabulary.** Point to people in the picture and talk about their abilities.
  He can fix a car.

- **Grammar.** Write polite requests.
  Could you please do the laundry?

- **Social language.** Create conversations for the people.
  A: Could you do me a favor?
  B: Sure. What?

Apartment 3A

Apartment 2C

Apartment 1A

✔ **Now I can . . .**

- ☐ discuss abilities.
- ☐ decline an invitation.
- ☐ request help or permission.

115

Past, Present, and Future Plans

UNIT GOALS

1 Get to know someone's life story
2 Announce good news and bad news
3 Ask about free-time activities

LESSON

1

Get to Know Someone's Life Story

A 🎧 **VOCABULARY.** Birth and childhood. **Listen and practice.**

1. be born

2. grow up

3. go to school

4. move

5. study

6. graduate

B 🎧 **LISTENING COMPREHENSION.** Listen to the conversation about Miyuki Sato's life. Then listen again and check ☑ the statements that are true.

1. ☐ Miyuki Sato was born in Japan.
2. ☐ Her father worked in Peru.
3. ☐ She grew up in Peru.
4. ☐ Miyuki speaks Chinese.
5. ☐ The family never moved to Japan.

C **PAIR WORK.** Interview your partner. Write the answers.

1. When were you born? _____

2. Where were you born? _____

3. Where did you grow up? _____

D 🎧 **PRONUNCIATION.** Diphthongs. **Listen and practice.**

1. /aɪ/	**2.** /aʊ/	**3.** /ɔɪ/
die	how	boy
I	house	Roy
time	noun	oil
tie	town	boil

E 🎧 **VOCABULARY.** Academic subjects. **Listen and practice.**

1. architecture

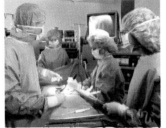

2. medicine

3. psychology

4. business

5. education

6. mathematics / math

7. science

8. nursing

9. engineering

10. law

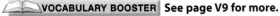

VOCABULARY BOOSTER See page V9 for more.

CONVERSATION • *Get to know someone's life story.*

1. 🎧 **MODEL. Read and listen.**

Elena: Where were you born?

Sam: In New York.

Elena: And did you grow up there?

Sam: Yes, I did. And you?

Elena: I was born in Brasilia. I grew up in Toronto.

Sam: Toronto? That's interesting. Why did you move there?

Elena: My parents are Canadian.

2. 🎧 **Rhythm and intonation practice**

3. PAIR WORK. Now exchange real information. Start like this:

A: Where were you born?

B: In _____.

Continue in your <u>own</u> way . . .

NEED HELP? Here's language you already know:

What do you do?
What are you studying now?
Where did you study?
Did you graduate?
What did you study?

Announce Good News and Bad News

A 🎧 VOCABULARY. More life events. Listen and practice.

1. get married   2. get divorced   3. have children   4. live happily ever after   5. die

B GRAMMAR. Would like

She **would like to have** two children.
I'd like to study architecture.

> I would like → **I'd like**

Would you **like to have** children?   Yes, I **would**. / No, I **wouldn't**.
What **would** he **like to study**?   Chinese.

C WHAT ABOUT YOU? Complete the survey. Then, on a separate piece of paper, write statements with <u>would like</u>.

> *I'd like to have children in the next two years.*

What would you like to do in the next two years?

☐ get married   ☐ move to a new apartment or house   ☐ meet a good-looking man
☐ graduate   ☐ study a new language   ☐ meet a good-looking woman
☐ have children   ☐ write a book   ☐ meet a Scorpio
☐ move to a new country   ☐ learn to play a musical instrument   ☐ paint my living room
☐ move to a new city   ☐ get a new boss   ☐ buy a new refrigerator

Scoring: Give yourself 1 point for each check mark.
   0-5 points: Time to do something new!
   6-10 points: Wow! Sounds like you have an interesting life.
   11-15 points: Relax! You're going to do too much.

MYSELF Magazine

D PAIR WORK. Compare your survey with a partner's.

GRAMMAR. <u>Be going to</u> for the future

Next year, I**'m going to have** a baby.
He**'s going to move** to Italy.

Are you **going to study** architecture?	Yes, I am. / No, I'm not.
Who**'s going to graduate** tomorrow?	Jeannette.
When **are** you **going to have** children?	I don't know.

F **Write questions or statements with <u>be going to</u>.**

1. Where / you study ___*Where are you going to study*___?

2. My sister / have a baby / in September _____.

3. When / they get married _____?

4. My neighbor / get divorced _____.

5. My brother and I / study medicine _____.

CONVERSATION • *Announce good news and bad news.*

1. 🎧 **MODEL.** **Read and listen.**

Tom: Hi, Scott. What's new?
Scott: Well, I have some great news.
My daughter is going to have a baby.
Tom: Congratulations!
Scott: Thanks.

2. 🎧 **Rhythm and intonation practice**

3. PAIR WORK. **Now role-play a conversation about good news or bad news.**

A: Hi, _____. What's new?
B: Well, I have some _____ news. _____.
A: _____ . . .

Continue in your <u>own</u> way . . .

🎧 **Responses to good news**
• Congratulations!
• I'm so happy for you.
• I'm so happy to hear that.
• Best wishes!

🎧 **Responses to bad news**
• I'm sorry.
• Oh no. I'm sorry.
• I'm so sorry to hear that.
• That's too bad. I'm so sorry.

Ask about Free-time Activities

A 🎧 **VOCABULARY.** Free-time activities. **Listen and practice.**

1. travel

2. go camping

3. go fishing

4. relax

5. hang out with friends

6. sleep late

7. do nothing

Also remember
- exercise • paint
- go running • read
- go to the beach

📖 **VOCABULARY BOOSTER** See page V9 for more.

B 🎧 **LISTENING COMPREHENSION.** Listen. Complete each statement. Then listen again to check your work.

1. He's going to ___go camping___ .

2. She's going to _____ .

3. They're going to _____ .

4. She's going to _____ .

5. He's going to _____ .

6. He's going to _____ .

C **GRAMMAR.** Conditions and results in the future

if- clause [condition]	future result
If the weather **is** nice,	**I'm going to go** to the beach.
If the weather **isn't** nice,	**I'm going to sleep** late.

Always use the present tense in the if- clause.

If she **has** enough time, she's going to see the movie again. NOT If she ~~is going to have~~ enough time . . .

An if- clause can come at the beginning of the sentence or at the end.

If **she stays home**, she's going to relax. OR She's going to relax **if she stays home**.

Complete the conditional sentences.

1. If we _____ enough money, we're going to travel this summer.
   have / are having

2. If there is enough time, they _____ a vacation.
   take / are going to take

3. If Mark _____ his ticket today, the concert is going to be very expensive.
   doesn't buy / isn't buying

4. If Carla and Ed _____ married, they're going to have lots of children.
   are going to get / get

5. She _____ to Paris if she gets divorced.
   's going to move / moves

6. If you don't leave now, you _____ late.
   're going to be / are

7. I'm not going to clean the house tomorrow if it _____ too hot.
   going to be / is

8. What are you going to do if you _____ enough time this summer?
   have / having

E **PAIR WORK.** **Ask and answer the following questions. Then, on a separate piece of paper, write about your partner.**

1. If the weather is nice this weekend, what are you going to do?

2. If you have enough time today, what are you going to do?

3. If you have enough money, where are you going to go?

CONVERSATION • *Ask about free-time activities.*

1. 🎧 **MODEL. Read and listen.**

Pam: What do you like to do in your free time?

Katy: Well, I like to hang out with friends.

Pam: So, are you going to do that this weekend?

Katy: Maybe.

3. PAIR WORK. Now make small talk with your partner. Use the pictures for ideas.

A: What do you like to do in your free time?

B: Well, I like to _____.

A: So, are you going to do that _____?

B: _____.

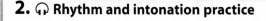

2. 🎧 **Rhythm and intonation practice**

TOP NOTCH
ACTIVITIES

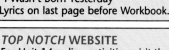

TOP NOTCH SONG
"I Wasn't Born Yesterday"
Lyrics on last page before Workbook.

TOP NOTCH WEBSITE
For Unit 14 online activities, visit the
Top Notch Companion Website at
www.longman.com/topnotch.

A **READING. Read and listen to the article.
Then answer the questions.**

Thor Heyerdahl, Explorer

SOUTHEAST ASIA

Pacific Ocean

EASTERLY WIND

OCEAN CURRENTS

POLYNESIA

CALLAO, PERU

North

West · East

South

Thor Heyerdahl

The Kon-Tiki

Thor Heyerdahl was born in Norway in 1914. Heyerdahl got married in 1937. He and his wife, Liv, moved to Polynesia that year. While they lived there, Heyerdahl liked to go fishing. When he went fishing, he studied the wind and the Pacific Ocean currents.

In 1947, people thought that the first Polynesians had come from the west, from Southeast Asia. Because of the winds and the ocean currents, Heyerdahl had a different idea.

He thought the first Polynesians had come from the east.

In 1947, Heyerdahl made the Kon-Tiki, a raft of balsa wood. With a crew of men from many countries, he traveled 8000 kilometers [4300 miles] from Callao, Peru, to Polynesia. The voyage of the Kon-Tiki was very difficult. It took 101 days. But it proved that Heyerdahl's idea was possible. Heyerdahl died in 2002.

Information source: *Kon-Tiki: Across the Pacific by Raft* by Thor Heyerdahl (New York: Pocket Books, 1990)

1. What was Heyerdahl's occupation? *Thor Heyerdahl was an explorer* .

2. Where was he from? _____ .

3. When was he born? _____ .

4. When did he get married? _____ .

5. What was his wife's name? _____ .

6. Where did he move in 1937? _____ .

7. What did he study? _____ .

8. Where did he travel to in 1947? _____ .

9. **Challenge:** Why did Heyerdahl build the Kon-Tiki? _____ .

B **WHAT ABOUT YOU?** **On a separate piece of paper, write a short history of your life. Include a picture. Then tell your class about it.**

	I was born in 1980. I grew up in . . .

UNIT WRAP-UP

- Tell the story of Katherine Rudy's life in the past, present, and future. What did she do? What is she doing now? What would she like to do?

Katherine was born in 1981. She grew up in Chicago . . .

CHECKPOINT

A **LISTENING COMPREHENSION.** **Listen to the conversations and check** ☑
each statement <u>True</u> or <u>False</u>. Then listen again to check your work.

	True	False
1. She likes soup for breakfast.	☐	☐
2. She gets up early every day.	☐	☐
3. He makes the beds.	☐	☐
4. He often takes a nap.	☐	☐
5. She gets dressed before breakfast.	☐	☐
6. He takes the bus to work.	☐	☐

B **Write a sentence about each picture. Use the present continuous.**

1. _She's getting up_ .

4. _____ .

2. _____ .

5. _____ .

3. _____ .

6. _____ .

C PAIR WORK. Write questions about daily activities. Use <u>When</u>, <u>What time</u>, <u>How often</u>, and <u>Who</u>. Ask your partner the questions. Write your partner's answers.

Questions   Your partner's answers

What time do you get up ?   _7:00_ .

1. _____ ?   _____ .

2. _____ ?   _____ .

3. _____ ?   _____ .

4. _____ ?   _____ .

D GROUP WORK. Tell the class about your partner's daily activities.

❝Jack gets up at 7:00 every day.❞

E Complete each sentence with the simple present tense of the verb.

Let me tell you about life in my family. We all ____ at about 6:00. But
                                              1. get up
after that, everyone ____ a different routine. My mom ____ to work early,
                     2. have   3. go
and she ____ time for breakfast. So she ____ a quick cup of coffee and
        4. [not] have   5. drink
____ out the door. My father ____ at home. He ____ breakfast for the
6. run   7. work   8. make
family. He ____ into the kitchen at about 6:15 and ____ to music as
         9. go   10. listen
he ____ breakfast. After breakfast, my sisters ____ the school bus, but I
   11. cook   12. take
____ a little more time. I ____ the breakfast dishes, ____ my teeth, ____
13. have   14. wash   15. brush   16. comb
my hair, and then I ____ to school. On Saturdays, my mom ____ the house,
                    17. walk   18. clean
and my dad ____ the laundry. On the weekend, we make our beds in the
           19. do
morning. From Monday to Friday, we ____ time to make our beds.
                                   20. [not] have

PAIR WORK • Exchange real information about your typical day.

Start like this: What's your typical week like?

💡 *Ideas*

Talk about:
• household chores
• daily activities
• weekdays / weekends

F Write the present participle of each of the following verbs.

1. write ___writing___
2. make _____
3. wear _____
4. watch _____
5. shop _____

6. get up _____
7. have _____
8. do _____
9. drive _____
10. study _____

G Write the activity. Use the present continuous.

1.  ___He's shaving___.

2.  _____.

3.  _____.

4.  _____.

5.  _____.

6.  _____.

7.  _____.

8.  _____.

H Choose a response to each statement or question. Circle the letter.

1. "How often do you walk to work?"
   a. Three times a week.   b. Yes, I walk to work.

2. "What are you doing this weekend?"
   a. I go to the park.   b. I'm not sure.

3. "Want to get together?"
   a. No wonder I never see you.   b. Sorry, I can't. I'm too busy.

4. "Please pass the butter."
   a. Here you go.   b. Actually, I don't like butter.

5. "Can you play the guitar?"
   a. No, I can't.   b. I can't. I'm a morning person.

6. "Could you please hand me that book?"
   a. Maybe some other time.   b. Sure.

7. "My daughter's going to get married."

    a. I'm sorry. I'm too busy.   **b.** That's great!

8. "Should I call you back later?"

    a. Yes, please. I'm feeding the kids. **b.** I can't. I'm making lunch.

9. "What's wrong?"

    a. I have a terrible cold.   **b.** You should take something.

 **PAIR WORK.** Write your <u>own</u> response to each statement or question. Then practice your exchanges with a partner.

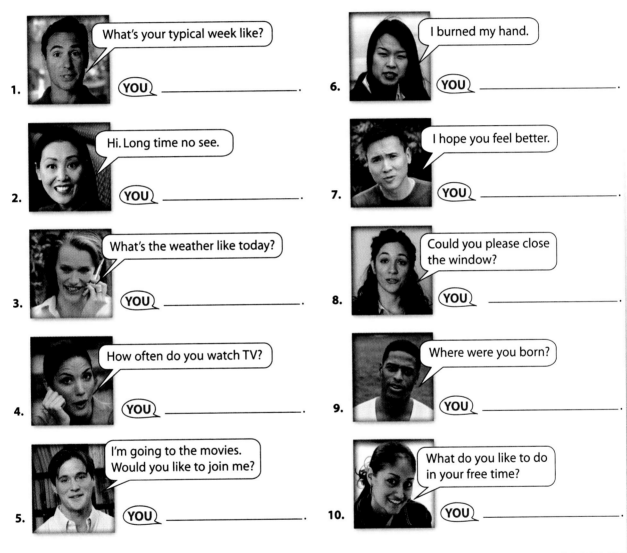

1. What's your typical week like?   (YOU) _____.

2. Hi. Long time no see.   (YOU) _____.

3. What's the weather like today?   (YOU) _____.

4. How often do you watch TV?   (YOU) _____.

5. I'm going to the movies. Would you like to join me?   (YOU) _____.

6. I burned my hand.   (YOU) _____.

7. I hope you feel better.   (YOU) _____.

8. Could you please close the window?   (YOU) _____.

9. Where were you born?   (YOU) _____.

10. What do you like to do in your free time?   (YOU) _____.

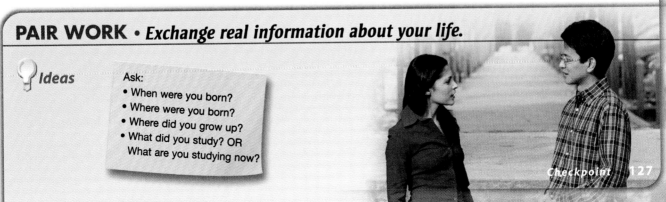

PAIR WORK • *Exchange real information about your life.*

Ideas

Ask:
- When were you born?
- Where were you born?
- Where did you grow up?
- What did you study? OR What are you studying now?

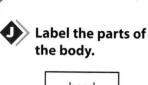

J **Label the parts of the body.**

head
finger
chest
ankle
arm
foot
hip
leg
shoulder
hand

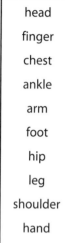

1. _____
2. _____
3. _____
4. _____
5. _____
6. _____
7. _____
8. _____

9. _____
10. _____

K **Write statements and questions about the future. Use <u>be going to</u>.**

1. This weekend / they / see a great movie _This weekend they're going to see a great movie_.
2. When / you / make the beds _____?
3. What / he / study _____?
4. I / have/ four children _____.
5. you / take a vacation this summer _____?

L **Underline the base form of the verb in the following sentences.**

1. I can <u>write</u> English but I can't <u>speak</u> English.
2. Do you like coffee for breakfast?
3. What do you do?
4. I'm going to take a nap.

5. They can't go to the train station at 3:00.
6. You should see a doctor.
7. Could you please open the door?
8. He shouldn't go to work today.

M **Write the name of each container.**

1. a _____ of soda

2. a _____ of tea

3. a _____ of potatoes

4. a _____ of juice

N ▷ PAIR WORK. Look at the pictures.
Ask your partner questions about his or her table.

> 66 Are there any apples on your table? 99
>
> 66 No, there aren't. 99

PARTNER A

PARTNER B

◈ ▷ Write the ingredients for a recipe you know.

Recipe: _____
Ingredients:
_____
_____
_____
_____
_____

P ▷ Complete each statement or question with the correct form of the verb.

1. I never _____ a jacket.
   <small>wear / am wearing</small>
2. I _____ white shirts.
   <small>like / am liking</small>
3. Who _____ a suit today?
   <small>wears / is wearing</small>
4. How many sweaters do you _____ for your trip?
   <small>need / needing</small>
5. This afternoon we _____ shopping.
   <small>going / 're going</small>

PAIR WORK • *Exchange real information about your plans for the future.*

Start like this: What would you like to do in the next year?

 Ideas
- move
- graduate
- have children
- get married

Q ⬧ Suggest a remedy for each person in the pictures. Use <u>should</u> or <u>shouldn't</u>.

1. *You should take something*   .

4. _____.

2. _____.

5. _____.

3. _____.

6. _____.

R ⬧ Check ☑ the statements or questions that are in the simple present tense.

☑ **1.** I speak English well.

☐ **2.** Do you like bananas?

☐ **3.** I was born in 1983.

☐ **4.** Who does the dishes in your house?

☐ **5.** She had a bad cold.

☐ **6.** They went to Europe on their vacation.

☐ **7.** I'm going to get married today.

☐ **8.** What do you do?

☐ **9.** What are you doing?

☐ **10.** Where were you this morning?

S ⬧ 🎧 **LISTENING COMPREHENSION. Listen to the conversations. Check ☑ <u>Past</u>, <u>Present</u>, or <u>Future</u>. Then listen again to check your work.**

	Past	Present	Future
1.	☐	☑	☐
2.	☐	☐	☐
3.	☐	☐	☐
4.	☐	☐	☐
5.	☐	☐	☐
6.	☐	☐	☐

T ▸ **Write a question for each response.**

1. **A:** <u>Would you like coffee or tea</u>_____?
   B: Me? I'd like coffee, please.

2. **A:** _____?
   B: I'd like to go to Italy.

3. **A:** _____?
   B: I was born in New York.

4. **A:** _____?
   B: Yes, I ski very well.

5. **A:** _____?
   B: Me? I'm a morning person.

6. **A:** _____?
   B: I'm going to study German.

7. **A:** _____?
   B: I broke my arm!

U ▸ **Complete each sentence with a form of <u>be</u> or <u>have</u>.**

1. My daughter _____ long, blonde hair.

2. My parents _____ both short.

3. Salma Hayek _____ beautiful.

4. What color eyes _____ your children _____?

5. I _____ not very tall and not very short.

V ▸ **GROUP WORK.** On a separate piece of paper, write a physical description of yourself. Mix papers with your classmates. Then, guess who wrote each description.

> I am tall. I have straight, brown hair.

PAIR WORK • *Exchange real information about a good or bad vacation.*

💡 *Ideas*

Ask:
• When did you go?
• Where did you go?
• What happened?

Alphabetical word list for Fundamentals A and B

This is an alphabetical list of all productive vocabulary in the ***Top Notch Fundamentals*** units. The numbers refer to the page on which the word first appears or is defined. When a word has two meanings, both are in the list. Entries for Fundamentals A are in black. Entries for Fundamentals B are in blue.

A

a 4
a lot of 54
A.M. 36
abdomen 102
ability 109
academic subject 117
across 20
across from 52
across the street 20
activity 68
actor 6
actress 18
actually 49
add 90
address 16
affirmative 4
after 68
afternoon 41
ago 92
ailment 104
airport 24
alphabet 8
always 72
an 4
ankle 102
any 84
apartment 52
apple 84
appliance 56
April 40
architect 4
architecture 117
arm 102
around the corner 20
around the corner from 52
article 4
artist 4
at 41
athlete 6
August 40
autumn 96
awful 57

B

back 102
backache 104
badly 109
bag 87
balcony 52
bald 100
ball 74
banana 84
bank 20
banker 4
baseball 42

base form 94
bath 68
bathroom 54
bathtub 56
be 4
be going to 119
beach 95
beans 84
beard 100
beautiful 48
beautifully 109
bed 56
bedroom 54
before 68
better 105
between 52
bike riding 95
birth 116
birthday 40
black 48
blonde 100
blouse 44
blue 48
boat 98
body 102
boil 90
bookcase 56
bookstore 20
born 116
boss 12
bottle 87
bowl 90
box 87
bread 86
break 102
breakfast 68
brother 28
brown 48
brush 68
building 52
burn 102
bus 22
bus station 22
business 117
busy 71
butter 86

C

cabbage 90
cabinet 56
calendar 39
camping 120
can *n.* 87
can *v.* 108
can't 108
car 108
cell phone 17

chair 56
check *v.* 70
cheese 86
chef 6
chest 102
chicken 86
child 28
childhood 116
chin 100
chop 90
chore 70
city, cities 36
class 37
classmate 12
clean *adj.* 48
clean *v.* 70
close 112
closet 54
clothes 44
cloudy 76
coffee 86
cold 76
colleague 12
color 48
comb 68
come 69
come home 68
common noun 9
community 20
computer 56
concert 38
congratulations 119
container 87
contraction 4
convenience store 20
cook 90
cool 76
corner 20
cough 104
could 112
count noun 84
crawl 114
cup 90
curly 100
cut 102
cute 32

D

daily 68
dance 108
dancing 73
dark 100
date 40
daughter 28
day 38
day after tomorrow 80

December 40
definitely 69
dentist 104
describe 32
descriptive adjective 48
desk 56
die 118
dining room 54
dinner 73
directions 20
dirty 48
dish 70
divorced 118
do 70
doctor 4
door 52
down 20
downstairs 54
down the street 20
drain 90
draw 108
dress 44
dressed 68
dresser 56
drink 86
drive *n.* 95
drive *v.* 24

E

ear 100
earache 104
early 37
easy chair 56
eat 68
education 117
egg 84
elevator 52
e-mail 70
engineer 4
engineering 117
evening 41
evening person 69
event 38
every 70
every day 70
exercise 70
expensive 110
explorer 122
eye 100
eyebrow 100
eyelash 100

F

face 100
factory 52
fall *v.* 102

fall *n.* 96
fall down 102
familiar 101
family 28
family member 28
father 28
favor 113
February 40
feed 79
feel 105
fever 104
few 114
finger 102
fingernail 102
first 40
first floor 52
first name 14
fish 86
fishing 120
fix 108
flight attendant 4
floor 52
food 84
foot 102
free time 120
freezer 56
frequency adverb 72
Friday 38
fridge 85
friend 12
furniture 56

G

game 38
garage 52
garbage 70
garden 52
garlic 90
get 68
get up 68
glasses 112
go 22
good-looking 32
go out 73
go to bed 68
graduate 116
grandchild 28
granddaughter 28
grandfather 28
grandmother 28
grandparent 28
grandson 28
gray 48
great 57
green 48
grow up 116

stadium 24
stairway 52
stomach 102
stomachache 104
stove 56
straight 22
straight (hair) 100
street 20
student 4
study 116
subject pronoun 6
sugar 86
suit 44
summer 96
Sunday 38
sunny 76
sweater 44
swim 108
swimming 95

T
table 56
tablespoon 90
take 24
take a bath 68
take a nap 70
take a shower 68
take a taxi 24
take out the garbage 70
take something 104

take the bus 24
take the train 24
tall 32
taxi 22
taxi stand 22
tea 86
teacher 4
teeth 68
telephone 56
temperature 76
terrible 57
terribly 109
that 44
their 12
there are 54
there is 21
these 44
they 6
thin 90
thing 89
third 40
third floor 52
this 44
this (afternoon) 80
those 44
throw 114
Thursday 38
tie 44
time 36
tired 110

title 14
today 80
toe 102
toenail 102
toilet 56
tomato 84
tomorrow 80
tongue 100
tonight 80
too 110
tooth 100
toothache 104
train 22
train station 22
transportation 25
travel 120
travel agency 20
Tuesday 38
turn left 22
turn off 112
turn on 112
turn right 22
TV 56
twice 70
typical 71

U
ugly 57
undressed 68
upstairs 54
usually 72

V
vacation 97
very 32
violin 108

W
wake 94
walk *n.* 95
walk *v.* 24
want 46
warm 76
was 92
wash 70
wash the dishes 70
watch TV 68
water 86
wavy 100
we 6
wear 94
weather 76
Wednesday 38
week 38
weekday 38
weekend 38
well 109
were 92
what 16
what day 38
what time 38
when 38

where 21
white 48
who 29
wife 28
window 52
windy 76
winter 96
wishes 119
woman 28
word 114
workplace 52
would like 87
write 94
writer 6

Y
year 40
yellow 48
yes 7
yes / no question 46
yesterday 92
you 6
young 32
your 12

Z
zero 16
Zodiac sign 42

Social language list for Fundamentals A and B

Welcome to *Top Notch!*

Hi.
Hello.
I'm [Martin].
Nice to meet you [too].
Glad to meet you.
It's a pleasure to meet you.
Good morning.
Good afternoon.
Good evening.

How's everything?
How's it going?
How are you?
[I'm] fine, thanks.
Great.
Not bad.
So-so.
And you?
I'm fine.

Good-bye.
Bye-bye.
See you later.
Take care.
Good night.
See you tomorrow.
OK.

Unit 1

What do you do?
I'm [a banker].
And you?
Excuse me. (to initiate a conversation)
Are you [Marie]?

No, I'm not. / Yes, I am.
Right over there.
Thank you.
You're welcome.
Hello.

I'm [John Bello].
Excuse me? (to ask someone to repeat)
How do you spell that?

Unit 2

[Tom], this is [Paula].
[Paula]'s my [classmate].
What's your [last name], please?

And your [first name]?
My [first name]? (to ask for clarification)
What's your phone number?

That's right.

Unit 3

Where's [the bookstore]?
It's [down the street].
Is there a [bank] near here?
Yes.
There's a [bank] [down the street].

How do I get to the [train station]?
Turn [right] at the corner.
Go straight.
Go to the corner of [Main Street] and
  [Park Avenue].

Go [two] blocks and turn [left].
No problem.
Don't [walk].
Take [the bus].

Unit 4

Who's that?
That's [my father].
And who are [they]?
[They're] my [sisters], [Julie] and [Trish].

I have [one brother] and [two sisters].
Really?
How old [is] your [brother]?
Tell me about [your father].

Well, [he]'s a [doctor].
[He]'s very [tall].
And how about [your mother]?

Unit 5

What time is it?
It's [one o'clock].
What time is [English class]?
Uh-oh. (to express dismay)
Am I late?
No, you're not.
Don't worry.

You're on time.
What day is the [party]?
There's a [play] on [Tuesday].
Would you like to go?
Sounds great.
What time?
OK. (to express willingness)

Let's meet at [a quarter to seven].
When's [your birthday]?
On [July 15th].
When's yours?
My birthday's in [November].

Unit 6

I like that [dress].
Do you like this [sweater]?
Yes, I do. / No, I don't.

Actually, I think [it's] [very nice].
Let's go shopping.
What do you need?

I need [a tie] and [a new suit].
Is that all?

Unit 7

I [study] at [the Park School].
Where's that?
On [Second Street].
Near [the mall].
Do you live nearby?
What about you?

Me?
I [work] at [Peter's Restaurant].
Do you live in a house or an apartment?
What's it like?
Well, there are [three bedrooms] and
  [a large kitchen].

Sounds nice.
Look at that [easy chair].
What do you think?
You do?
Definitely.
I'm not sure.

Unit 8

Are you a morning person or an evening
  person?
I'm definitely [an evening person].
Why do you say that?
I get up [after ten].

I go to bed [after two].
What's your typical [week] like?
On [Mondays] and [Wednesdays] I [go
  to school].
Sounds like you're pretty busy.

Long time no see.
Do you always [take the bus]?
I usually [walk].
No wonder I never see you!

Unit 9

What's the weather like?
I'm calling from [San Francisco].
How's the weather in [Buenos Aires]?
Awful.
No kidding.
It's [hot and sunny] here.
Hello? (to answer the telephone)

This is [Laura].
What are you doing?
Should I call you back later?
Talk to you later.
Bye.
So, what are you doing [this weekend]?
If the weather is [good], I'm [meeting
  Andrea in the park].

Do you want to get together [on
  Sunday]?
I'm not doing anything special.
Sure. (to express willingness)
Call me [Sunday morning].

Unit 10

How about some [tomato potato soup]?
That sounds [delicious]!
I love [tomatoes].
[Are] there any [potatoes] [on the shelf]?
Do we have any [tomatoes]?
I'll check.

Would you like [coffee] or [tea]?
I'd like [coffee], please.
No, thanks.
Please pass the [butter].
Here you go.
Hey, [Alison].

Would you like to join me?
What are you [drinking]?
Mmm.
I think I'd like [the same thing].

A4

Unit 11

Where were you [yesterday]?	Pretty good, thanks.	Yes, I was.
When?	What did you do last weekend?	I just got back [last week].
I was [at home].	Not much.	How was it?
There was a great [party] at [the Pike Museum].	I [went running].	Really nice.
There was?	About the same.	It's great to see you.
Too bad I wasn't there!	You look [great].	Welcome back.
	Were you on vacation?	

Unit 12

Who's that?	That's [Daniela Mercury].	I feel [awful].
[She] look[s] familiar.	[She]'s a [singer] from [Brazil].	What's wrong?
Who?	What happened?	You really should [take something].
The [woman] with [long, curly, blonde] [hair].	I [broke] my [ankle].	Good idea.
	I'm sorry to hear that.	I hope you feel better.

Unit 13

Can you [swim]?	Not at all.	That's too bad.
Can you?	I'm really sorry.	Maybe some other time.
I [swim] [very well].	I'm too busy.	Could you do me a favor?
When did you learn?	I don't feel well.	Could you please [close the window]?
When I was [about eight].	It's too late.	
Was it hard?	I have other plans.	

Unit 14

Where were you born?	Why did you move there?	My [daughter] is going to [have a baby].
I was born in [New York].	My parents are [Canadian].	Congratulations.
And did you grow up there?	What's new?	What do you like to do in your free time?
That's interesting.	I have some [great] news.	

Countries and nationalities

Country	Nationality	Country	Nationality	Country	Nationality
Argentina	Argentinian / Argentine	France	French	Peru	Peruvian
Australia	Australian	Germany	German	The Philippines	Filipino
Bolivia	Bolivian	Greece	Greek	Poland	Polish
Brazil	Brazilian	Guatemala	Guatemalan	Russia	Russian
Canada	Canadian	Indonesia	Indonesian	Saudi Arabia	Saudi / Saudi Arabian
Chile	Chilean	Ireland	Irish	Spain	Spanish
China	Chinese	Japan	Japanese	Switzerland	Swiss
Colombia	Colombian	Korea	Korean	Thailand	Thai
Costa Rica	Costa Rican	Lebanon	Lebanese	Turkey	Turkish
Ecuador	Ecuadorian	Malaysia	Malaysian	The United Kingdom	British
Egypt	Egyptian	Mexico	Mexican	The United States	American
El Salvador	El Salvadoran	New Zealand	New Zealander	Venezuela	Venezuelan
England	English	Panama	Panamanian	Uruguay	Uruguayan

Numbers 100 to 1,000,000,000

100	one hundred	10,000	ten thousand
500	five hundred	100,000	one hundred thousand
1,000	one thousand	1,000,000	one million
5,000	five thousand	1,000,000,000	one billion

Verb list

This is an alphabetical list of all active verbs in the *Top Notch Fundamentals* units.
The page numbers refer to the page on which the base form of the verb first appears.

base form	simple past	page
be	was / were	4
ride	rode	95
break	broke	102
brush	brushed	68
burn	burned	102
can	could	108
check	checked	70
clean	cleaned	70
close	closed	112
comb	combed	68
come	came	69
cut	cut	102
dance	danced	108
die	died	118
do	did	70
draw	drew	108
drive	drove	24
eat	ate	68
exercise	exercised	70
fall	fell	102
feed	fed	79
feel	felt	105
fix	fixed	108

base form	simple past	page
get	got	68
go	went	22
graduate	graduated	116
grow	grew	116
hand	handed	112
hang out	hung out	120
have	had	30
help	helped	112
hurt	hurt	102
knit	knitted	108
laugh	laughed	114
lie	lay	104
like	liked	45
listen	listened	70
live	lived	118
make	made	73
move	moved	116
mow	mowed	74
need	needed	46
open	opened	112
paint	painted	108
pass	passed	87
pick up	picked up	114

base form	simple past	page
play	played	70
put	put	90
read	read	70
relax	relaxed	120
ride	rode	94
see	saw	94
sew	sewed	108
shave	shaved	68
ski	skied	108
sleep	slept	120
spell	spelled	9
study	studied	116
swim	swam	108
take	took	24
travel	traveled	120
turn	turned	22
wake	woke	94
walk	walked	24
want	wanted	46
wash	washed	70
watch	watched	68
wear	wore	94
write	wrote	94

Pronunciation table

These are the pronunciation symbols used in *Top Notch Fundamentals*.

Vowels		Consonants			
Symbol	Key Words	Symbol	Key Words	Symbol	Key Words
i	feed	p	park, happy	ʃ	she, station, special, discussion
ɪ	did	b	back, cabbage		
eɪ	date, table	t	tie	ʒ	leisure
ɛ	bed, neck	d	die	h	hot, who
æ	bad, hand	k	came, kitchen, quarter	m	men
ɑ	box, father	g	game, go	n	sun, know
ɔ	wash	tʃ	chicken, watch	ŋ	sung, singer
oʊ	comb, post	dʒ	jacket, orange	w	week, white
ʊ	book, good	f	face, photographer	l	light, long
u	boot, food, student	v	vacation	r	rain, writer
ʌ	but, mother	θ	thing, math	y	yes, use, music
ə	banana, mustache	ð	then, that		
ɚ	shirt, birthday	s	city, psychology		
aɪ	cry, eye	z	please, goes		
aʊ	about, how	t̬	butter, bottle		
ɔɪ	boy	t̚	button		
ɪr	here, near				
ɛr	chair				
ɑr	guitar, are				
ɔr	door, chore				
ʊr	tour				

FUNDAMENTALS B

VOCABULARY BOOSTER

UNIT 8

🎧 More household chores

1. dust

2. sweep

3. mop

4. vacuum

UNIT 9
🎧 More weather

1. a thunderstorm

2. a snowstorm

3. a hurricane

4. a tornado

UNIT 10
🎧 More vegetables

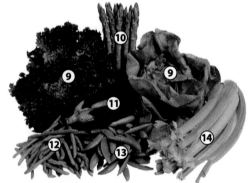

1. carrots
2. cabbage
3. broccoli
4. cauliflower
5. leeks
6. cucumbers
7. brussels sprouts

8. corn

9. lettuce
10. asparagus
11. an eggplant
12. beans
13. peas
14. celery

15. garlic

🎧 More fruits

1. a tangerine
2. a grapefruit
3. a lemon
4. a lime
5. an orange

6. grapes
7. a pineapple
8. bananas

9. a pear

10. apricots

11. peaches

12. strawberries

13. raspberries

14. a honeydew melon
15. an avocado
16. a papaya
17. a mango
18. a kiwi

19. a watermelon

20. raisins
21. figs
22. prunes
23. dates

UNIT 11
🎧 More weekend activities

1. go horseback riding

2. go sailing

3. play golf

4. go rollerblading

5. go snorkeling

6. go rock climbing

7. go ice skating

8. go windsurfing

UNIT 12

🎧 **More parts of the body**

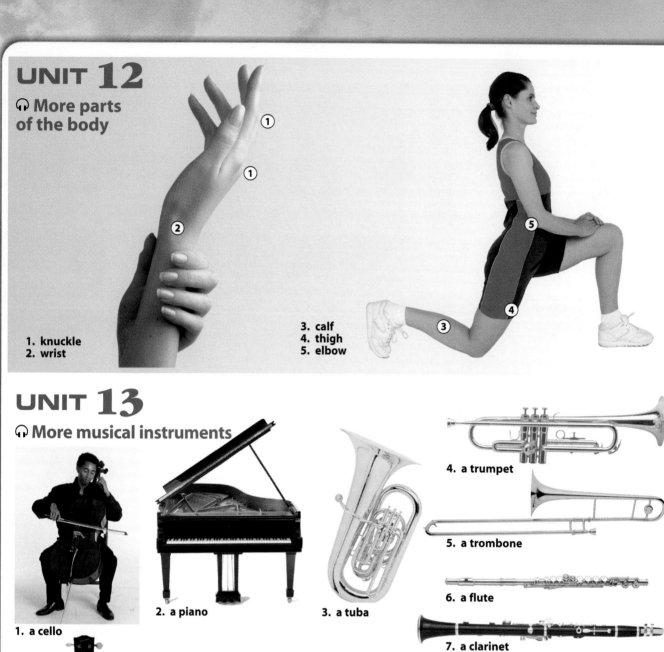

1. knuckle
2. wrist
3. calf
4. thigh
5. elbow

UNIT 13

🎧 **More musical instruments**

1. a cello

2. a piano

3. a tuba

4. a trumpet

5. a trombone

6. a flute

7. a clarinet

8. a recorder

9. a guitar

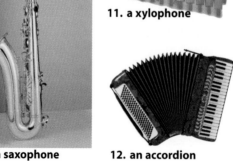

10. a saxophone

11. a xylophone

12. an accordion

13. drums

UNIT 14

More academic subjects

1. biology

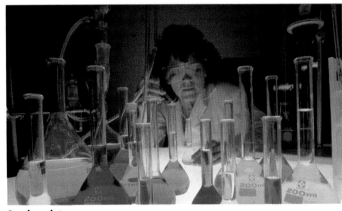

2. chemistry

3. history

4. fine art

5. drama

More free-time activities

1. go skiing

2. go hiking

3. play

4. garden

5. go on a cruise

6. get a manicure

🎧 *TOP NOTCH POP* LYRICS FOR FUNDAMENTALS A AND B

Excuse Me, Please [Unit 2]

(CHORUS)

Excuse me—please excuse me.
What's your number?
What's your name?
I would love to get to know you,
and I hope you feel the same.

I'll give you my e-mail address.
Write to me at my dot-com.
You can send a note in English
so I'll know who it came from.

Excuse me—please excuse me.
Was that 0078?
Well, I think the class is starting,
and I don't want to be late.

But it's really nice to meet you.
I'll be seeing you again.
Just call me on my cell phone
when you're looking for a friend.

(CHORUS)

So welcome to the classroom.
There's a seat right over there.
I'm sorry, but you're sitting in
our teacher's favorite chair!

Excuse me—please excuse me.
What's your number?
What's your name?

Tell Me All about It [Unit 4]

Tell me about your father.
He's a doctor and he's very tall.
And how about your mother?
She's a lawyer. That's her picture on
    the wall.

Tell me about your brother.
He's an actor, and he's twenty-three.
And how about your sister?
She's an artist. Don't you think she looks
    like me?

(CHORUS)

Tell me about your family—
who they are and what they do.
Tell me all about it.
It's so nice to talk with you.

Tell me about your family.
I have a brother and a sister, too.
And what about your parents?
Dad's a teacher, and my mother's eyes
    are blue.

(CHORUS)

Who's the pretty girl in that photograph?
That one's me!
You look so cute!
Oh, that picture makes me laugh!
And who are the people there, right below
    that one?
Let me see … that's my mom and dad.
They both look very young.

(CHORUS)

Tell me all about it.
Tell me all about it.

On the Weekend [Unit 8]

(CHORUS)

On the weekend,
when we go out,
there is always so much joy and laughter.
On the weekend,
we never think about
the days that come before and after.

He gets up every morning.
Without warning, the bedside clock rings
    the alarm.
So he gets dressed—
he does his best to be on time.
He combs his hair, goes down the stairs,
and makes some breakfast.
A bite to eat, and he feels fine.
Yes, he's on his way
to one more working day.

(CHORUS)

On Thursday night,
when he comes home from work,
he gets undressed, and if his room's a mess,
he cleans the house. Sometimes he takes
    a rest.
Maybe he cooks something delicious,
and when he's done
he washes all the pots and dishes,
then goes to bed.
He knows the weekend's just ahead.

(CHORUS)

My Favorite Day [Unit 11]

Last night we walked together.
It seems so long ago.
And we just talked and talked.
Where did the time go?

We saw the moonlit ocean
across the sandy beach.
The waves of summer fell,
barely out of reach.

(CHORUS)

Yes, that was then,
and this is now,
and all I do is think about
yesterday,
my favorite day of the week.

When I woke up this morning,
my feelings were so strong.
I put my pen to paper,
and I wrote this song.

I'm glad I got to know you.
You really made me smile.
My heart belonged to you
for a little while.

(CHORUS)

It was wonderful to be with you.
We had so much to say.
It was awful when we waved good-bye.
Why did it end that way?

(CHORUS)

I Wasn't Born Yesterday [Unit 14]

I went to school and learned the lessons
of the human heart.
I got an education in
psychology and art.

It doesn't matter what you say.
I know the silly games you play.

(CHORUS)

I wasn't born yesterday.
I wasn't born yesterday.

Well, pretty soon I graduated
with a good degree.
It took some time to understand
the way you treated me,

and it's too great a price to pay.
I've had enough, and anyway,

(CHORUS)

So you think I'd like to marry you
and be your pretty wife?
Well, that's too bad, I'm sorry, now.
Grow up and get a life!

It doesn't matter what you say.
I know the silly games you play.

(CHORUS)

TOP NOTCH   FUNDAMENTALS   B

Workbook

Joan Saslow ■ Allen Ascher

with Julie C. Rouse

PEARSON
Longman

Activities

LESSON 1

1 YOUR MORNING ACTIVITIES. Put the activities in order. Write ordinal numbers (1ˢᵗ, 2ⁿᵈ, . . .) on the lines. Write an X next to the activities you don't do.

_____ take a shower / a bath

_____ eat breakfast

_____ put on my makeup

_____ get up

_____ shave

_____ get dressed

_____ brush my teeth

_____ comb / brush my hair

Choose your first three morning activities. What time do you do them?

1. _____ .

2. _____ .

3. _____ .

2 Write the room where you do each activity.

1. take a shower / a bath: _in the bathroom_ _____

2. get dressed: _____

3. comb / brush my hair: _____

4. eat dinner: _____

5. watch TV: _____

6. study: _____

3 Look at the activities and the times. Write sentences in the simple present tense.

1. _She comes home at 6:30_____ .   2. _____ .

3. _____ .   4. _____ .

4 Write the name of a family member or friend. Check ✔ his or her activities.

Name: _____

☐ takes a shower in the evening   ☐ studies after dinner

☐ takes a shower in the morning   ☐ watches TV after dinner

☐ doesn't eat breakfast   ☐ gets up early on the weekend

☐ eats a big breakfast   ☐ gets up late on the weekend

Now write sentences about this person.

5 Complete the conversation.

Are you a morning person or an evening person?

1. **YOU** _____.

Why do you say that?

2. **YOU** _____.

LESSON 2

6 Look at the pictures. Then write sentences about the household chores Mr. and Mrs. Rand do.

Mr. Rand

1. _Mr. Rand washes the dishes_____.

2. _____.

3. _____.

Mrs. Rand

4. _____.

5. _____.

6. _____.

7 Look at Lawrence's weekly schedule.

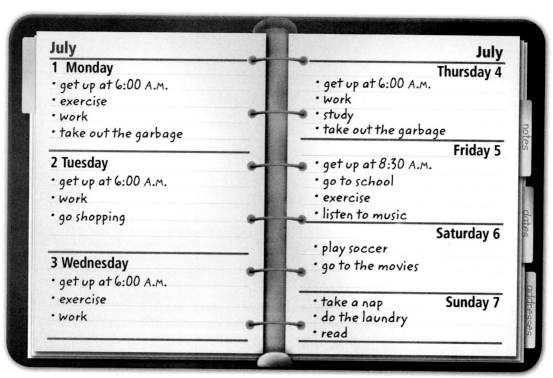

July

1 Monday
- get up at 6:00 A.M.
- exercise
- work
- take out the garbage

2 Tuesday
- get up at 6:00 A.M.
- work
- go shopping

3 Wednesday
- get up at 6:00 A.M.
- exercise
- work

July

Thursday 4
- get up at 6:00 A.M.
- work
- study
- take out the garbage

Friday 5
- get up at 8:30 A.M.
- go to school
- exercise
- listen to music

Saturday 6
- play soccer
- go to the movies

Sunday 7
- take a nap
- do the laundry
- read

notes   dates   addresses

Now complete the sentences about Lawrence.

1. Lawrence _____ once a week.

2. He _____ twice a week.

3. He _____ three times a week.

4. He _____ four days a week.

5. On Fridays, he _____.

6. On Friday evenings, he _____.

7. On the weekend, he _____.

8 Look at Lawrence's weekly schedule again. Complete the conversation between Alicia and Lawrence.

1. **Alicia:** What's your typical week like?

   Lawrence: _____.

2. **Alicia:** And what about Fridays?

   Lawrence: _____.

3. **Alicia:** What do you do on the weekend?

   Lawrence: _____.

4. **Alicia:** Sounds like you're pretty busy. When do you do your chores?

   Lawrence: _____.

LESSON 3

9 How often do you ...? Check ✔ <u>always</u>, <u>usually</u>, <u>sometimes</u>, or <u>never</u>.

	always	usually	sometimes	never
1. eat breakfast	☐	☐	☐	☐
2. watch TV in the evening	☐	☐	☐	☐
3. go to bed before 11:00 P.M.	☐	☐	☐	☐
4. take a bath	☐	☐	☐	☐
5. read before bed	☐	☐	☐	☐
6. exercise in the morning	☐	☐	☐	☐
7. make the bed	☐	☐	☐	☐
8. wash the dishes after dinner	☐	☐	☐	☐
9. listen to music at home	☐	☐	☐	☐
10. take a nap	☐	☐	☐	☐

10 WHAT ABOUT YOU? **Answer the questions.**

1. What do you do every day? _____.

2. What do you do twice a day? _____.

3. Where do you usually eat lunch? _____.

4. What do you usually do after dinner on weekdays? _____.

5. What do you do about once a week? _____.

6. What do you do on Friday nights? _____.

11 **Write sentences about the daily activities or weekly schedule of a family member or a friend.**

Example: *My brother always goes to the movies on Fridays.* _____

_____

_____

_____

_____

JUST FOR **FUN**

1 **A RIDDLE FOR YOU!**

What comes once in an afternoon, twice in a week, but never in a day or a month?
(Hint: It comes once in the alphabet.)

Answer: _____

2 WORD FIND. **Look across (→) and down (↓). Circle the seven household chores or work activities and the seven leisure activities. Then write the chores / work activities and leisure activities on the lines.**

W	A	T	C	H	T	V	U	C	E	A	K	A	U	H	I	T
E	P	N	A	C	O	H	C	L	H	S	O	I	K	V	R	I
K	L	W	A	S	H	T	H	E	D	I	S	H	E	S	E	A
G	A	L	M	S	G	A	N	A	M	C	T	M	N	M	A	M
E	Y	L	M	G	O	A	L	N	K	B	A	O	H	A	D	K
T	S	O	R	O	D	T	N	T	S	D	K	W	W	K	W	O
V	O	A	G	T	A	A	T	H	A	A	E	T	N	E	V	O
A	C	E	D	O	N	S	C	E	U	N	A	H	I	D	A	I
C	C	S	A	W	C	Y	H	H	O	M	B	E	A	I	W	I
U	E	N	U	O	I	C	S	O	E	U	A	L	O	N	H	E
U	R	S	R	R	N	B	T	U	T	E	T	A	D	N	S	E
M	L	N	S	K	G	E	G	S	O	O	H	W	A	E	A	E
C	H	C	B	D	O	T	H	E	L	A	U	N	D	R	Y	D
T	E	L	I	S	T	E	N	T	O	M	U	S	I	C	H	D
T	E	T	A	K	E	A	N	A	P	E	N	H	A	O	I	E
L	H	T	I	A	K	N	T	T	U	E	W	W	N	S	S	A

SOURCE: Created with www.spellbuilder.com

Chores / Work Activities

_____

_____

_____

_____

_____

_____

_____

Leisure Activities

_____

_____

_____

_____

_____

_____

_____

Riddle: the letter e

UNIT 9

Weather and Ongoing Activities

LESSON 1

1 What's the weather like? Is it hot, cold, warm, or cool?

1. _____

2. _____

3. _____

4. _____

 Look at the pictures. What are the people doing right now? Write sentences in the present continuous.

1. *She's brushing her teeth* _____ .

2. _____ .

3. _____ .

4. _____ .

5. _____ .

6. _____ .

3 Look at the pictures. Answer the questions. Use a short answer and the present continuous.

1. Is he taking a bath?   *No, he isn't. He's taking a shower.* _____

2. Is she reading? _____

3. Are they listening to music? _____

4. Is she wearing a dress? _____

5. Is it snowing? _____

4 Where's Andrea? What's she doing? Match the places with Andrea's activities.

1. _____ She's in the kitchen.   **a.** She's going to bed.

2. _____ She's in the bedroom.   **b.** She's checking her e-mail.

3. _____ She's in the bathroom.   **c.** She's eating dinner with her family.

4. _____ She's in the dining room.   **d.** She's reading in the easy chair.

5. _____ She's in the office.   **e.** She's brushing her teeth.

6. _____ She's in the living room.   **f.** She's making breakfast.

LESSON 2

5 Look at the Ryan family's living room. Then read the answers and write questions about the family's activities. Use the present continuous.

1. **A:** _Where's the grandfather taking a nap_ ? **B:** On the sofa.

2. **A:** _____ ? **B:** Washing the dishes.

3. **A:** _____ ? **B:** They're going to a concert.

4. **A:** _____ ? **B:** The son is.

5. **A:** _____ ? **B:** An apple.

6. **A:** _____ ? **B:** Playing.

6 Imagine a really great day. Answer the questions in complete sentences.

1. Where are you? _____.

2. Who's there? _____.

3. What are you doing? _____.

4. What's the weather like? _____.

5. What are you wearing? _____.

7 Write the present participles.

1. take _____   6. do _____

2. play _____   7. drive _____ _____

3. study _____   8. call _____

4. exercise _____   9. go _____

5. eat _____   10. get dressed _____

LESSON 3

8 ▷ **Write the time, date, month, or year.**

1. right now: _____

2. today: _____

3. tomorrow: _____

4. the day after tomorrow: _____

5. this month: _____

6. this year: _____

9 ▷ **WHAT ABOUT YOU? Answer the questions in the present continuous.**

1. What are you doing today? _____.

2. What are you doing tonight? _____.

3. What are you doing tomorrow? _____.

4. What are you doing tomorrow evening? _____.

5. What are you doing this weekend? _____.

10 ▷ **Respond to the instant messages with your <u>own</u> information. Create your <u>own</u> screen name.**

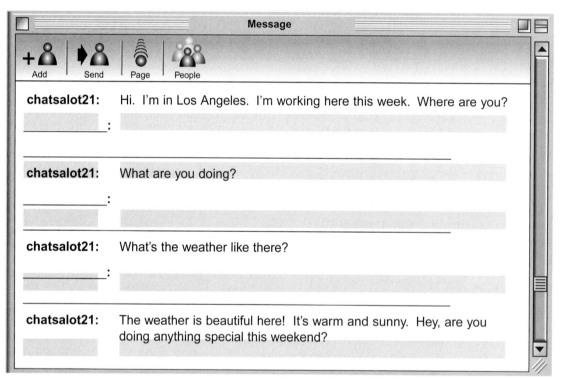

chatsalot21: Hi. I'm in Los Angeles. I'm working here this week. Where are you?

_____ : _____

_____

chatsalot21: What are you doing?

_____ :

_____

chatsalot21: What's the weather like there?

_____ :

_____

chatsalot21: The weather is beautiful here! It's warm and sunny. Hey, are you doing anything special this weekend?

11 ▷ **Write your plans for next week. Write sentences in the present continuous.**

JUST FOR FUN

1 Complete the puzzle. First, unscramble the letters of the time expressions. Then write the letters in the numbered boxes in the other boxes with the same number.

Time expressions

1. GITHR ONW

R I G H T N O W
  31 33 10   18

2. YOADT

[ ][ ][ ][ ][ ]
16   8 23

3. NTTOHGI

[ ][ ][ ][ ][ ][ ][ ]
24 13   7

4. TISH NMRINGO

[ ][ ][ ][ ]   [ ][ ][ ][ ][ ][ ]
36   5   25   21

5. TSHI NATRONFEO

[ ][ ][ ][ ]   [ ][ ][ ][ ][ ][ ][ ][ ]
      27   39 2   22 38 32 34

6. HITS GENNIVE

[ ][ ][ ][ ]   [ ][ ][ ][ ][ ][ ]
      41   3   26

7. OMTORWOR

[ ][ ][ ][ ][ ][ ][ ][ ]
35   28   6

8. TEH YDA TFREA TOOWORRM

[ ][ ][ ]   [ ][ ][ ]   [ ][ ][ ][ ][ ]   [ ][ ][ ][ ][ ][ ][ ]
    12   11 17   29   37   9   19

9. STIH EEKW

[ ][ ][ ][ ]   [ ][ ][ ][ ]
15   1   30

10. TISH MOTHN

[ ][ ][ ][ ]   [ ][ ][ ][ ]
4 14   40   20

Puzzle

" L [ ][ ]   [ ][ ]   [ ][ ][ ][ ]   [ ][ ] P P [ ][ ][ ]   [ ][ ]   [ ][ ] U
  1 2 3   4 5   6 7 8 9   10 11   12 13 14   15 16   17 18

[ ][ ] L [ ]   [ ][ ] U ' [ ][ ]   [ ] B U [ ] Y [ ][ ][ ][ ][ ][ ]
19 20 21 22   23 24   25 26   27   28 29 30 31 32 33

[ ][ ][ ][ ][ ]   P L [ ][ ][ ] . "
34 35 36 37 38   39 40 41

—John Lennon, singer and musician (U.K.)

SOURCE: Created with Discovery's Puzzlemaker.

TAKE A GUESS! **Match the weather and the places.**

1. _____ Number 1 hot place in the world
2. _____ Number 1 cold place in the world
3. _____ Number 1 rainy place in the world
4. _____ Number 1 snowy place in the world
5. _____ Number 1 sunny place in the world
6. _____ Number 1 cloudy place in the world

a. Plateau Station, Antarctica
b. Eastern Sahara Desert, Africa
c. Ben Nevis, Scotland
d. Mount Baker, Washington, U.S.A.
e. Cherrapunji, India
f. Dallol, Ethiopia

Guess: 1. f; 2. a; 3. e; 4. d; 5. b; 6. c

UNIT 10

Food

LESSON 1

1 Complete the chart. Check ☑ the boxes.

	oranges	bananas	eggs	tomatoes	apples	lemons	peas	peppers	potatoes	beans	onions
I like											
I don't like											
I have in my kitchen											
I need											
I eat every day											
I sometimes eat											
I never eat											

2 Look at the recipe.

Vegetable Omelet

Ingredients:

3 potatoes

6 eggs

1 small tomato

1/2 an onion

1/2 a pepper

Now answer the questions.

1. Are there any potatoes in the omelet? _____.

2. How many eggs are there? _____.

3. Are there any onions? _____.

4. How many tomatoes are there in the omelet? _____.

5. Which ingredients do <u>you</u> have for this recipe? _____.

6. Which ingredients do <u>you</u> need? _____.

3 ▷ Write questions with <u>How many</u>. Then answer the questions.

   1. students / your English class: _How many students are there in your English class_ ?
   _____ .

   2. people / your family: _____ ?
   _____ .

   3. days / this month: _____ ?
   _____ .

   4. sweaters / your closet: _____ ?
   _____ .

   5. bathrooms / your home: _____ ?
   _____ .

LESSON 2

4 ▷ Count or non-count? Write <u>a</u>, <u>an</u>, or <u>X</u> before each food or drink.

   1. _____ tea   5. _____ egg   9. _____ cheese
   2. _____ rice   6. _____ sugar   10. _____ lemon
   3. _____ banana   7. _____ oil   11. _____ juice
   4. _____ meat   8. _____ apple   12. _____ onion

5 ▷ Do you keep these foods in the fridge? On the shelf? On the counter?
   Write four sentences.

I keep soup, pasta, and sugar on the shelf.

juice	bread	milk
rice	butter	eggs
oil	tomatoes	tea

   1. _____ .
   2. _____ .
   3. _____ .
   4. _____ .

6 ▷ What color is it? What color are they? Write sentences.

   1. milk: _Milk is white_ .
   2. eggs: _____ .
   3. butter: _____ .
   4. orange juice: _____ .
   5. tomatoes: _____ .
   6. coffee: _____ .

7 **Label the pictures.**

1. _a loaf of bread_

2. _____

3. _____

4. _____

5. _____

8 **Write five sentences. Use words or phrases from each box.**

How many How much Is there any Are there any	**+**	meat juice oranges sugar bananas onions bread cans of soup	**+**	in the fridge? are there on the counter? do we have? is there? on the shelf? do you want? are there? in the kitchen?

1. _Are there any oranges in the fridge?_
2. _____
3. _____
4. _____
5. _____
6. _____

9 Look at the picture.

Complete the questions with <u>How much</u> or <u>How many</u>. Then answer the questions.

1. A: _____ peppers are there?   B: _____.

2. A: _____ water is in the fridge?   B: _____.

3. A: _____ bags of beans are there?   B: _____.

4. A: _____ soda is there?   B: _____.

10 Look at the picture in Exercise 9 again. Complete the questions with <u>Are there any</u> or <u>Is there any</u>. Then answer the questions.

1. A: _____ cheese in the fridge?   B: _____.

2. A: _____ eggs?   B: _____.

3. A: _____ juice?   B: _____.

4. A: _____ butter?   B: _____.

11 What's for dinner? Answer the questions in a restaurant.

1. "Would you like tomato soup or onion soup?"

    YOU _____.

2. "And would you like chicken or meat?"

    YOU _____.

3. "Would you like potatoes or brown rice?"

    YOU _____.

4. "Would you like coffee or tea later?"

    YOU _____.

5. "And then would you like an apple or an orange?"

    YOU _____.

LESSON 3

 12 **Complete each sentence. Circle the letter.**

1. Dr. Roberts _____ his e-mail every day.

   a. check   **b.** checks   **c.** is checking

2. Theresa _____ the laundry on Mondays.

   a. do   **b.** does   **c.** is doing

3. Lucas and Nate aren't at home. They _____ soccer in the park.

   a. play   **b.** plays   **c.** are playing

4. I _____ chicken with peppers for dinner. Would you like to join me?

   a. make   **b.** makes   **c.** am making

5. Mr. and Mrs. Juster usually _____ meat.

   a. doesn't eat   **b.** don't eat   **c.** aren't eating

13 **Complete the conversations. Use the simple present tense or the present continuous.**

1. **A:** What _____ right now?
   <u>you / eat</u>

   B: Chicken soup.

2. **A:** _____ milk in his coffee?
   <u>he / want</u>

   B: No, he doesn't. But he would like sugar.

3. **A:** What _____ in the fridge?
   <u>we / have</u>

   B: Soda, cheese, and an apple.

4. **A:** I _____ a dress to the party on Friday. How about you?
   <u>wear</u>

   B: I never _____ dresses.
   <u>wear</u>

5. **A:** _____ on Saturdays?
   <u>Jeff / work</u>

   B: Yes, usually. But this Saturday he _____ soccer.
   <u>play</u>

6. **A:** Where _____ lunch on Tuesdays?
   <u>you / eat</u>

   B: At Eli's Café. But today we _____ to City Bistro for my boss's birthday.
   <u>go</u>

JUST FOR FUN

 A RIDDLE FOR YOU!

George, Helen, and Steve are drinking coffee. Bart, Karen, and Dave are drinking soda.
Is Ellie drinking coffee or soda?
(Hint: Look at the letters in each drink.)

Answer: _____

SOURCE: <u>able2know.com</u>

 Complete the puzzle.

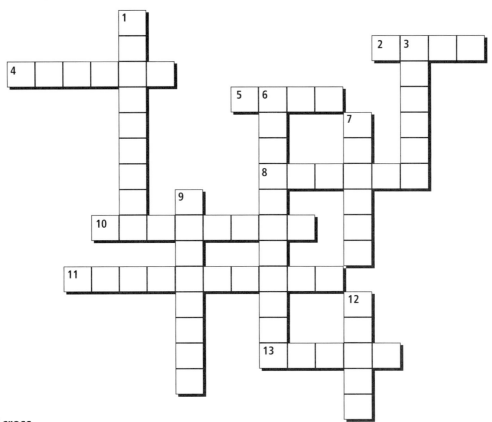

Across

2. A _____ of bread
4. Salt and _____
5. In Asia, people eat a lot of _____.
8. Directions for cooking something
10. You make this drink with lemons, water, and sugar.
11. A box, a bottle, a bag, and a can are all _____.
13. I like coffee with milk and _____.

Down

1. The place for milk: ____ ____
3. Would you like apple juice, _____ juice, or tomato juice?
6. The foods in a recipe
7. Water, tea, and soda are all _____.
9. In the omelet, there are three _____.
12. Peppers, peas, and _____ are green.

SOURCE: Created with Discovery's Puzzlemaker.

Riddle: Ellie is drinking coffee.

Past Events

LESSON 1

1 **Write the date, month, or year.**

1. yesterday: _____

2. last Wednesday: _____

3. three days ago: _____

4. one week ago: _____

5. last month: _____

6. two months ago: _____

7. last year: _____

8. five years ago: _____

2 **Complete the questions with <u>was</u> or <u>were</u>. Then answer the questions.**

1. Where _<u>were</u>_ you last night at 9:00? _<u>I was at home</u>_ _____.

2. _____ you at school yesterday? _____.

3. How _____ the weather last week? _____.

4. _____ there milk in your refrigerator this morning? _____.

5. What _____ your first e-mail address? _____.

6. When _____ your birthday? _____.

7. How old _____ you in 1996? _____.

8. Who _____ your favorite singer in the nineties? _____.

LESSON 2

3 **Complete the paragraph. Use the simple past tense forms of the verbs in the box. Use each verb only once.**

be	eat	put	wake
come	get	see	not exercise
drive	go	take	not read

Amy _____ home late last night. She and her colleagues _____ a movie after work.
     1.   2.

After the movie, they _____ out for dinner. This morning Amy _____ up at 8:00.
                              3.   4.

She usually wakes up at 7:00. She _____ a shower and _____ dressed by 8:10.
                                                      5.   6.

She usually takes the bus to work, but today she _____. In the car, she _____
                                                                              7.   8.

on her makeup and _____ a banana for breakfast. She _____, and she _____
                                 9.   10.   11.

the newspaper. But Amy _____ only five minutes late to work.
                                       12.

4 Write five sentences about your activities this morning. Look at the pictures for ideas.

5 Which activities do you like? Number the activities from 1 to 6 in the order you like to do them.

_____ go to the beach

_____ go swimming

_____ go for a walk

_____ go running

_____ go bike riding

_____ go for a drive

Which activity did you do? Which activity didn't you do? Write three sentences about <u>yesterday</u>, <u>last week</u>, and <u>last month</u>.

Examples: *I went to the beach yesterday* .

I didn't go bike riding last week .

1. _____ .

2. _____ .

3. _____ .

6 Write three things you did last weekend. Write three things you **didn't** do.

What I did

1. _____ .
2. _____ .
3. _____ .

What I didn't do

4. _____ .
5. _____ .
6. _____ .

LESSON 3

7 Circle the seasons where you live. Then write the months in each season where you live.

spring: _____

summer: _____

fall: _____

winter: _____

8 What's the weather usually like? Write the seasons where you live. Then check ✔ the weather where you live.

Seasons	cloudy	windy	sunny	cold	hot	warm	cool

9 WHAT ABOUT YOU? **Answer the questions.**

1. Did you eat breakfast this morning? _____.

2. Where did you eat lunch yesterday? _____.

3. How many books did you read last month? _____.

4. Where did you live five years ago? _____.

5. What time did you come home last night? _____.

6. Did you go to any movies last month? What did you see? _____

_____.

7. How often did you watch TV last week? _____.

8. What did you do last summer? _____.

10 Read the postcard from Luke's vacation.

Hello from Guatemala!

I'm in Antigua, Guatemala. I'm studying
Spanish. I go to class every morning, and
every afternoon there's an activity. On
Monday, we rode bikes to a coffee farm.
On Tuesday, there was a Latin dance
class. On Wednesday, we took a bus to
Chichicastenango and shopped in the
market. Yesterday we went to a
Guatemalan restaurant for lunch. Now
I'm in the ancient Mayan city of Tikal
for the weekend. It's beautiful.
Thinking of you!

Luke

Now look at the answers and write questions in the simple past tense.

1. A: _____? B: To Guatemala.

2. A: _____? B: He studied Spanish.

3. A: _____? B: Every morning.

4. A: _____? B: On Tuesday.

5. A: _____? B: He took a bus.

6. A: _____? B: In a restaurant.

Write a postcard about your last vacation. Answer five or more questions in the box.

When was it?	Where did you go?
What did you see?	What did you do?
What did you really like?	What did you <u>not</u> like?
How was the weather?	What did you eat?

Dear _____ ,

_____

_____

_____

_____

_____

_____

_____

Choose the correct words to complete the conversation. Write the letter on the line.

1. **A:** Hi, how's it going?

   B: _____

2. **A:** I was on vacation. I just got back yesterday.

   B: _____

3. **A:** I went to Hawaii for ten days.

   B: _____

4. **A:** Really nice.

   B: _____

5. **A:** I went to the beach every day. I went swimming and snorkeling. And I went sightseeing.

   B: _____

   A: Thanks!

a. What did you do?

b. Where did you go?

c. Pretty good. Hey, where were you last week?

d. Sounds wonderful. It's great to see you. Welcome back.

e. How was it?

JUST FOR **FUN**

1 ▷ **A RIDDLE FOR YOU!**

Where is the only place that yesterday always comes after today?
(Hint: Think of a book.)

Answer: _____

SOURCE: www.didyouknow.cd

2 ▷ **WORD FIND. Look across (→) and down (↓). Circle the base forms of the 20 verbs.
Then write the simple past tense forms of those verbs on the lines.**

H	A	V	E	Y	E	H	Y	K	K	E	R	R	T	K	A	E	L	E
E	C	G	E	Y	L	P	K	L	E	N	U	I	A	K	N	T	W	S
C	S	E	E	I	E	P	C	C	P	V	I	D	W	W	D	A	R	I
T	A	I	A	A	A	W	A	B	O	H	Y	E	C	M	T	L	I	L
T	O	N	A	T	R	T	D	L	E	C	U	E	H	N	E	K	T	O
E	E	W	E	A	R	A	H	I	I	P	A	E	E	T	I	A	E	E
L	A	O	T	L	Y	K	R	S	W	R	D	T	C	W	A	K	E	I
V	A	R	N	L	D	E	E	T	O	A	S	A	K	L	O	V	E	I
V	T	E	B	H	R	Y	D	E	T	C	D	R	I	V	E	T	I	I
E	Y	A	L	T	I	P	R	N	T	T	W	E	W	A	I	E	O	V
A	N	D	G	R	A	L	D	L	E	I	A	E	I	E	L	K	H	I
T	Y	N	C	A	E	A	K	E	L	C	S	L	M	V	S	E	W	H
C	H	E	H	W	E	Y	A	G	K	E	H	W	A	T	E	C	R	V
A	R	K	L	T	A	I	A	E	W	R	E	T	K	I	A	E	E	A
C	L	E	A	N	D	W	E	T	I	P	A	E	E	N	G	A	W	R
K	S	L	E	I	C	U	A	C	I	P	E	R	W	E	L	R	C	D

SOURCE: Created with www.spellbuilder.com

_____ _____ _____ _____

_____ _____ _____ _____

_____ _____ _____ _____

_____ _____ _____ _____

_____ _____ _____ _____

Riddle: In a dictionary

UNIT 12

Appearance and Health

LESSON 1

1 Check ✔ the adjectives that describe you.

1. My hair

☐ black ☐ blonde ☐ straight ☐ short

☐ brown ☐ gray ☐ wavy ☐ long

☐ red ☐ white ☐ curly ☐ bald

2. My eyes

☐ brown ☐ blue ☐ green

2 Describe a family member, a friend, or a colleague. Fill in the chart.

| Person | Hair | | | Eye color |
	color	straight, wavy, or curly	long, short, or bald	
My brother	blonde	straight	short	blue

3 Write the parts of the face.

eyebrow	nose
eye	mouth
eyelashes	chin
ear	neck

1. _____

2. _____

3. _____

4. _____

5. _____

6. _____

7. _____

8. _____

4▷ Look at Exercise 1 again. Use the information to write sentences with <u>be</u> about yourself.

Example: _My hair is brown_ .

1. _____ .

2. _____ .

3. _____ .

5▷ Look at Exercise 2 again. Use the information to write sentences with <u>have</u> about a family member, a friend, or a colleague.

Example: _My brother has blue eyes_ .

1. _____ .

2. _____ .

3. _____ .

6▷ Choose three famous people to describe.

Here's language you already know:

pretty	short
handsome	tall
good-looking	old
cute	young

1. _Nicole Kidman_ : _She's tall. She's pretty. She has long, curly, red hair._
Her eyes are blue. She's an actress from Australia.
_____
_____

2. _____ : _____
_____
_____
_____

3. _____ : _____
_____
_____
_____

4. _____ : _____
_____
_____
_____

LESSON 2

 7 **Write the parts of the body.**

1. _____

2. _____

3. _____

4. _____

5. _____

6. _____

7. _____

8. _____

head	neck	shoulder
chest	arm	hand
hip	leg	knee
ankle	foot	
stomach / abdomen		

9. _____

10. _____

11. _____

12. _____

8 **What happened? Write a sentence about each picture.**

1. *She burned her hand* _____ .

2. _____ .

3. _____ .

4. _____ .

5. _____ .

Now complete the conversation.

6. **A:** _____ ?

   B: I broke my leg.

7. **A:** _____ .

   B: Thanks!

LESSON 3

 9 Check ✔ the remedies for each ailment.

	take something	lie down	have some tea	see a doctor	see a dentist	don't go to work or school	eat	don't eat
a cold								
a fever								
a sore throat								
a stomachache								
a backache								
a toothache								

10 Think about an ailment you had. Then answer the questions.

> **Be careful:**
>
> <u>Lie</u> is irregular in the simple past tense:
>
> lie (down) ➡ lay (down)

1. What was wrong? _____.

2. What did you do? _____.

11 Your friend Brendan is going out with a colleague tonight. He wants your advice. Answer his questions.

1. Brendan: "We're going to the movies. What should we see?"

    YOU _____.

2. Brendan: "After the movie, we're going out for dinner. Where should we go?"

    YOU _____.

3. Brendan: "Should I talk about work?"

    YOU _____.

4. Brendan: "What should I wear?"

    YOU _____.

JUST FOR FUN

1 ▷ Complete the puzzle. First, unscramble the letters of the ailments. Then write the letters in the numbered boxes in other boxes with the same number.

Ailments

1. ONT ELEF LLEW ☐ N O T ☐ F E E L ☐ W E L L
   (17)   (19) (8)

2. A ODLC ☐ ☐☐☐☐
   (4)

3. A UOCHG ☐ ☐☐☐☐☐
   (7)

4. A RESO OTARHT ☐ ☐☐☐☐ ☐☐☐☐☐
   (10)   (13)

5. A SOACHHCAETM ☐ ☐☐☐☐☐☐☐☐☐☐
   (15)

6. A EEVFR ☐ ☐☐☐☐☐
   (1) (14)

7. A AADEECHH ☐ ☐☐☐☐☐☐☐
   (9) (6)

8. NA REAHEAC ☐☐ ☐☐☐☐☐☐
   (3) (16)

9. A KCABEACH ☐ ☐☐☐☐☐☐☐☐
   (12)   (18)

10. A OOTTHCHEA ☐ ☐☐☐☐☐☐☐☐
    (11)   (5)

11. A YNURN SEON ☐ ☐☐☐☐☐ ☐☐☐☐
    (20)   (2)

Puzzle

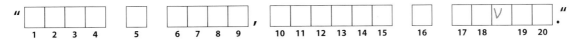

" ☐☐☐☐ ☐ ☐☐☐☐ , ☐☐☐☐☐☐ ☐ ☐☐V☐ . "
(1)(2)(3)(4) (5) (6)(7)(8)(9) (10)(11)(12)(13)(14)(15) (16) (17)(18) (19)(20)

—An old saying

Appearance and Health **W 7 5**

2 Complete the puzzle.

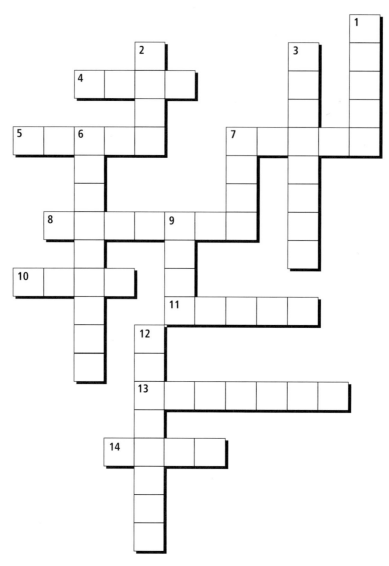

Across

4. It's between your hip and your ankle.
5. Hair on a man's chin
7. They're white. They're in your mouth.
8. They're on your hands. You have ten.
10. Parts of the body for shoes
11. Not long
13. Another word for "abdomen"
14. Doesn't have hair

Down

1. It's between your nose and your chin.
2. Part of the body for a hat
3. Take something, lie down, and have some tea are all _____.
6. Burn your finger, cut your hand, and fall down are all _____.
7. They're on your feet. You have ten.
9. What you use to see
12. Hair between a man's nose and mouth

Source: Created with Discovery's Puzzlemaker.

UNIT 13

Abilities and Requests

LESSON 1

1 Complete the chart. Check ✓ your abilities and skills.

	play the violin	play the piano	drive a car	speak English	cook fish	make onion soup	play soccer
I can . . .							
I can't . . .							

2 Complete the conversations with <u>can</u> or <u>can't</u> and the base form of a verb.

1. **A:** _____ you _____ English?

   B: Oh, yes, and I _____ _____ Spanish, too.

2. **A:** _____ you _____ my computer?

   B: Fix it? No. I _____ _____ cars but not computers.

3. **A:** _____ you _____ my picture?

   B: No. I'm an engineer, not an artist.

4. **A:** _____ you _____ a sweater for me?

   B: Sorry. I can sew, but I _____ _____.

5. **A:** _____ you _____ the violin?

   B: No, but I _____ _____ the guitar.

3 Write about four different people. Complete the sentences with <u>can</u> or <u>can't</u> and an ability or skill.

Example: My sister: _Anna can fix a car_____.

1. My teacher: _____.

2. My friend: _____.

3. My neighbor: _____.

4. My colleague: _____.

4 Which occupation is good for you? Take the *Top Notch* Skills and
Interests Survey.

Top Notch Skills and Interests Survey

SKILLS		Do very well	Do well	Do OK	Do poorly	Can't do
	1. paint	⬭	⬭	⬭	⬭	⬭
	2. draw	⬭	⬭	⬭	⬭	⬭
	3. dance	⬭	⬭	⬭	⬭	⬭
	4. swim	⬭	⬭	⬭	⬭	⬭
	5. drive	⬭	⬭	⬭	⬭	⬭
	6. play the violin	⬭	⬭	⬭	⬭	⬭
	7. ski	⬭	⬭	⬭	⬭	⬭
	8. fix a car	⬭	⬭	⬭	⬭	⬭
	9. cook	⬭	⬭	⬭	⬭	⬭
	10. sing	⬭	⬭	⬭	⬭	⬭

INTERESTS		Like a lot	Like	Like a little	Don't like
	1. go to concerts	⬭	⬭	⬭	⬭
	2. go to museums	⬭	⬭	⬭	⬭
	3. listen to music	⬭	⬭	⬭	⬭
	4. make dinner for friends	⬭	⬭	⬭	⬭
	5. exercise	⬭	⬭	⬭	⬭
	6. go running	⬭	⬭	⬭	⬭
	7. go bike riding	⬭	⬭	⬭	⬭
	8. go for a drive	⬭	⬭	⬭	⬭

RESULTS

**Look at your answers.
What do you do very well? What do you like to do a lot?**

Can you cook well? Do you like to make dinner for friends?	➡ Maybe you should be a chef.
Can you sing, dance, play the violin (guitar, piano, other instruments)? Do you like to go to concerts and listen to music?	➡ Maybe you should be a singer or musician.
Can you swim and ski? Do you like to exercise and go running and bike riding?	➡ Maybe you should be an athlete.
Can you draw and paint? Do you like to go to museums?	➡ Maybe you should be an artist.
Can you drive and fix a car? Do you like to go for a drive?	➡ Maybe you should be a mechanic.

According to the survey, what should you be? _____

Answer the questions.

What can you do?

Example: _I can knit_ .

1. _____ .

3. _____ .

5. _____ .

When did you learn?

Example: _About two years ago_ .

2. _____ .

4. _____ .

6. _____ .

LESSON 2

 Write sentences with <u>too</u> and an adjective.

1. She can't drive.

She's too young .

2. She can't watch TV.

_____ .

3. You can't wear that shirt.

_____ .

4. He doesn't want that suit.

_____ .

5. We can't go bike riding today.

_____ .

6. She can't drink this coffee.

_____ .

7 Your friend wants to get together, but you decline the invitations. Give reasons.

1. "Let's go for a drive."

   (YOU) _____.

2. "OK, let's go out for lunch."

   (YOU) _____.

3. "How about a movie?"

   (YOU) _____.

4. "Well, maybe some other time."

   (YOU) _____.

LESSON 3

 8 Match the problems with the requests. Write the letter on the line.

1. _____ I'm cold.
2. _____ I need to check my e-mail.
3. _____ It's too hot.
4. _____ I don't have any clean clothes.
5. _____ I can't read this.
6. _____ There isn't any milk.

a. Could you please do the laundry?

b. Could you please close the window?

c. Could you please turn on the computer?

d. Could you please go shopping?

e. Could you please open the window?

f. Could you please hand me my glasses?

 9 Mrs. Cole's boss is coming for dinner at 6:00. But look at the house!

Help Mrs. Cole ask her husband to help. Write polite requests with <u>could</u> or <u>can</u>.

1. _Could you please take out the garbage_ _____ ?

2. _____ ?

3. _____ ?

4. _____ ?

5. _____ ?

Choose the correct response. Circle the letter.

1. Can you sing?

   a. No, I can't. I sing terribly.   b. Not right now. I'm too busy.   c. No, thanks.

2. When did you learn to ski?

   a. I just got back.   b. The day after tomorrow.   c. Last winter.

3. Let's go shopping.

   a. I'm sorry to hear that.   b. I'm sorry. I have other plans.   c. That's too bad.

4. Could you do me a favor?

   a. Sure. What?   b. Was it hard?   c. How was it?

5. Could you please turn off the TV?

   a. Not at all.   b. Sure. No problem.   c. Maybe some other time.

 Answer the questions. Write about <u>your</u> abilities and skills.

- What can you do well?
- When did you learn?
- What do you do poorly?

JUST FOR FUN

1 **What can they do? Match the famous people with their abilities.**

Mikhail Baryshnikov

Michael Schumacher

1. _____ Daniela Mercury

2. _____ Adriana Fernandez

3. _____ Gabriel Garcia Marquez

4. _____ Mikhail Baryshnikov

5. _____ Madhur Jaffrey

6. _____ Serena Williams

7. _____ Michael Schumacher

a. He can write.

b. He can dance.

c. She can sing.

d. He can drive.

e. She can play tennis.

f. She can cook.

g. She can run.

2 **Complete the puzzle.**

Across

1. I'm going to bed. Could you please _____ _____ the light?

4. Make dinner

6. Not well

7. Luis Miguel can do this.

8. Speak a second language, play the violin, and knit are all _____.

10. I'm cold. Could you please _____ _____ my sweater?

Down

2. A baby can do this at three months.

3. You can do this when there's snow.

5. The shoes are size 35. She wears a 37. They're _____ _____.

8. Make clothes

9. You can do this at the beach.

Source: Created with Discovery's Puzzlemaker.

UNIT 14

Past, Present, and Future Plans

LESSON 1

1 Read about Yao Ming's life.

Yao Ming's Life Story

Yao Ming was born on September 12, 1980. He grew up in a small apartment in Shanghai, China, with his parents. They were both basketball players too—and tall! Their son is 2.26 meters (7 feet 5 inches). Yao doesn't have any brothers or sisters. When he was about nine, he went to the Youth Sports School in Shanghai. In China, he played for the Shanghai Sharks.

In 2002, Yao moved to the United States. Now he plays professional basketball for the Houston Rockets. Yao and his mother live in a four-bedroom house in Houston. Yao's mother cooks Chinese food for him. He's learning English, and he's learning to drive a car.

Now look at the answers and write questions.

1. A: _____? B: On September 12, 1980.

2. A: _____? B: In Shanghai, China.

3. A: _____? B: At the Youth Sports School.

4. A: _____? B: In 2002.

2 For each academic subject, write the occupation.

1. architecture: _____

2. nursing: _____

3. science: _____

4. education: _____

5. engineering: _____

6. medicine: _____

7. law: _____

3 Get to know a famous person's life story. Choose a famous person. Answer the questions. Use the Internet, books, and other information.

1. Person's name: _____

2. When was he / she born? _____.

3. Where was he / she born? _____.

4. Where did he / she grow up? _____.

5. Where did he / she go to school? _____.

6. What did he / she study? _____.

7. Did he / she graduate? When? _____.

8. What does he / she do now? _____.

LESSON 2

 4 What would you like to do in your life? Write four sentences. Look at the pictures and the verbs in the box for ideas.

 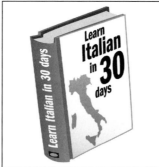 

move	have children	meet
study	go	see
graduate	learn	buy
get married		

Example: *I would like to go to Australia* _____.

1. _____.

2. _____.

3. _____.

4. _____.

5 ▸ Write your responses to good news and bad news.

1. "I'm going to graduate this year."

   (YOU) _____.

2. "My parents are going to get divorced."

   (YOU) _____.

3. "My grandfather died two days ago."

   (YOU) _____.

4. "My wife and I are going to have a baby."

   (YOU) _____.

5. "I met a nice, good-looking man. We're going to get married."

   (YOU) _____.

6. "I'm going to move to London for work. I don't want to go."

   (YOU) _____.

LESSON 3

6 ▸ What are you going to do this summer? Check ✔ the boxes.

☐ travel	☐ relax	☐ exercise
☐ go camping	☐ sleep late	☐ work
☐ go fishing	☐ do nothing	☐ go to school
☐ go bike riding	☐ hang out with friends	☐ move
☐ go to the beach	☐ go for walks	☐ get married

Now write to a friend about your plans. Write sentences with be going to.

Complete the conditional sentences, using <u>be going to</u>. Use real information.

1. If the weather is nice this weekend, _____.
2. If the weather isn't nice this weekend, _____.
3. If I have enough time this week, _____.
4. If I stay home tomorrow night, _____.
5. If I have enough money next year, _____.

Complete the conditional sentences. Use the present tense or <u>be going to</u>.

1. If it's warm tomorrow, I _____ to work.
   walk

2. If Matt _____, he's going to do poorly in this class.
   not study

3. We're going to buy shoes if we _____ to the mall.
   go

4. If Pamela takes a vacation this year, she _____.
   travel

5. They _____ a big family if they get married.
   have

6. Mr. and Mrs. Johnson are going to go out for dinner after the movie if it

   _____ too late.
   not be

9 A reporter from your school newspaper wants to write an article about you. Answer her questions about yourself.

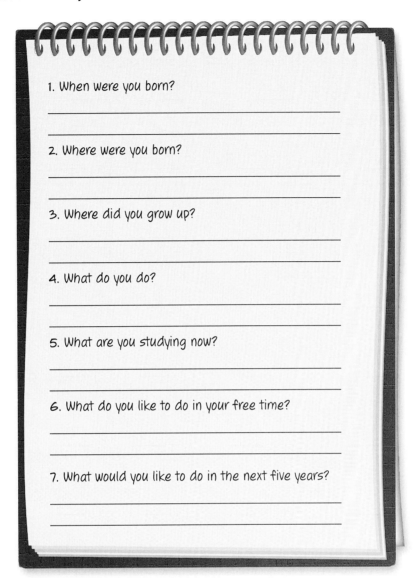

1. When were you born?
_____
_____

2. Where were you born?
_____
_____

3. Where did you grow up?
_____
_____

4. What do you do?
_____
_____

5. What are you studying now?
_____
_____

6. What do you like to do in your free time?
_____
_____

7. What would you like to do in the next five years?
_____
_____

JUST FOR FUN

 A RIDDLE FOR YOU!

When asked how old she was, Suzie answered, "In two years I'm going to be twice as old as I was five years ago." How old is she now?

a. Twelve.   **b.** Seven.   **c.** Fourteen.

 Complete the puzzle.

Across

2. Go places

5. Academic subject for teachers

8. Go to live in a new home: ____

10. A very young person

11. Become husband and wife: ____ ____

12. Complete school

Down

1. A response to good news

3. The name of Heyerdahl's raft

4. Academic subject for doctors

6. Architecture, psychology, and law are all ____ ____.

7. A response to bad news: ____ ____

9. Take a nap

Source: Created with Discovery's Puzzlemaker.

Riddle: a

CHECKPOINT

1 **WHAT ABOUT YOU?** **Answer the questions.**

1. How often should you brush your teeth?

   _____.

2. Can you check e-mail on your cell phone?

   _____.

3. Are you listening to music right now?

   _____.

4. Can you cook fish well?

   _____.

5. Are you going to go running if the weather is nice this weekend?

   _____.

6. Would you like to go to the beach this summer?

   _____.

7. Where did you go on your last vacation?

   _____.

8. Where would you like to go on your next vacation?

   _____.

9. What can't you do? Would you like to learn?

   _____.

10. What should you study if you want to make a lot of money?

   _____.

2 **WEATHER REPORTS.** **Check ✔ yesterday's weather.**

☐ cloudy   ☐ sunny   ☐ windy   ☐ cold

☐ hot   ☐ warm   ☐ cool

Now write sentences.

1. What was the weather like yesterday?

   _____.

2. What's the weather like today? Is it raining or snowing?

   _____.

3 **Read about Andrea Bocelli.**

He's an Italian opera singer, but people of all ages, young and old, listen to his music. He sings beautifully and is famous all over the world. He has dark, wavy hair and a beard. His name is Andrea Bocelli.

Bocelli was born on September 22, 1958 in Tuscany. He grew up on his family's farm. He started singing for family members when he was about three years old. When he was six, he

learned to play the piano. He can also play the flute and the saxophone. At the age of twelve, he had a soccer accident, and now he can't see. Bocelli graduated from the University of Pisa. He studied law, but he only worked for one year as a lawyer.

He started to study music. His teacher was the famous singer Franco Corelli. In the evenings, he sang in piano bars. During this time, he got married. He and his wife, Enrica, have two children, Amos and Matteo. In 1992, Luciano Pavarotti listened to a tape of Bocelli singing. This was good news for Bocelli's music career. Between 1994 and 2003, he made about 20 albums.

Bocelli lives in Monte Carlo. In the summer, he and his family live in Tuscany, where he grew up. Bocelli has a busy schedule. He studies music and practices singing for two hours or more every day. He travels a lot. He writes, too. He wrote a book about his life story, *The Music of Silence*. In his free time, he reads and cooks Italian food.

4 **To write this article, a reporter interviewed Andrea Bocelli. Answer the reporter's questions for Bocelli.**

1. **Reporter:** Where were you born?

   Bocelli: *I was born in Tuscany* _____.

2. **Reporter:** And did you grow up there?

   Bocelli: _____.

3. **Reporter:** What did you study?

   Bocelli: _____.

4. **Reporter:** Can you play any musical instruments?

   Bocelli: _____.

5. **Reporter:** When did you learn to play the piano?

   Bocelli: _____.

6. **Reporter:** Tell me about your family.

   Bocelli: _____.

7. **Reporter:** Where do you live now?

   Bocelli: _____.

8. **Reporter:** What is your daily schedule like?

   Bocelli: _____.

5 Look again at the article in Exercise 3. Circle all 19 simple past tense verbs in the article. Write 10 of these verbs on the lines. Then write the base form of the 10 verbs.

1. _was_   →   _be_
2. _____ → _____
3. _____ → _____
4. _____ → _____
5. _____ → _____

6. _____ → _____
7. _____ → _____
8. _____ → _____
9. _____ → _____
10. _____ → _____

OPTIONAL VOCABULARY BOOSTER ACTIVITIES

1 Check ✔ the weather where you live. Then write the season(s).

| In what season(s)? |

1. ☐ thunderstorms   _____
2. ☐ snowstorms   _____
3. ☐ hurricanes   _____
4. ☐ tornadoes   _____

2 Make a fruit or vegetable salad. Write the ingredients on the recipe card.

_____ **Salad**

Ingredients:

3 Check ✔ the activities you do. Then circle your three favorite activities.

☐ go rock climbing   ☐ get a manicure
☐ go rollerblading   ☐ go ice skating
☐ play golf   ☐ go sailing
☐ go snorkeling   ☐ go horseback riding

How often do you do your three favorite activities?

1. _____ .
2. _____ .
3. _____ .

4 **Circle the word or phrase that is different.**

1. grapefruit   (peach)   lemon   tangerine
2. dust   play   mop the floor   vacuum the house
3. go sailing   go snorkeling   go windsurfing   go rock climbing
4. knuckle   knee   calf   thigh
5. saxophone   flute   trumpet   drums
6. biology   drama   medicine   chemistry

 5 **You're going to go to a beach resort for five days. All activities are included. Look at the activities you can do.**

Sunset Vacations

Do you want to be busy every minute or just relax on the beach? Look at all our great activities and make your plans.

And don't worry about the weather. It's always beautiful. Have a wonderful vacation!

play volleyball on the beach
play golf
go bike riding
go horseback riding
go swimming
go snorkeling
go sailing

go windsurfing
go fishing
go on a boat ride
go water skiing
exercise
get a manicure
go shopping

take a taxi to a nearby town
have dinner on your balcony
go on a dinner cruise
go for a walk on the beach
go dancing
take a nap or sleep late
relax or do nothing!

Complete the chart. Plan your morning, afternoon, and evening activities for each day.

	Morning	Afternoon	Evening
Saturday			
Sunday			
Monday			
Tuesday			
Wednesday			

Now answer these questions about your plans.

1. What are you going to do on Saturday morning? _____
2. What are you going to do on Tuesday afternoon? _____
3. What are you doing on Wednesday evening? _____
4. Are you going to go snorkeling? When? _____
5. Are you going to go windsurfing? When? _____